READY-TO-GO GAME SHOWS (THAT TEACH SERIOUS STUFF)

Bible Edition

READY-TO-GO GAME SHOWS (THAT TEACH SERIOUS STUFF)

Bible Edition

Michael Theisen

Saint Mary's Press™

Genuine recycled paper with 10% post-consumer waste.
Printed with soy-based ink.

The publishing team included Brian Singer-Towns, development editor; Gabrielle Koenig, copy editor and production editor; Hollace Storkel, typesetter; Cindi Ramm, art director; Cären Yang, designer; C. J. Potter, illustrator; manufactured by the production services department of Saint Mary's Press.

The activities in this book are not formally associated with any trademarked television game show or board game, past or present.

Printed in the United States of America

Printing: 9 8 7 6 5 4

Year: 2009 08 07 06 05

ISBN 0-88489-689-7

Library of Congress Cataloging-in-Publication Data

Theisen, Michael.
     Ready-to-go game shows (that teach serious stuff) : Bible edition / Michael Theisen.
     p. cm.
ISBN 0-88489-689-7 (pbk.)
     1. Bible games and puzzles—Juvenile literature. [1. Bible games and puzzles.] I. Title.
GV1507.B5 T53 2001
220—dc21

                                        2001000870

This book is dedicated to Christopher Clark McDermott—
classmate, roommate, best friend, best man, godfather, "Uncle,"
and superior game show host.
And that's my final answer!

Special Thanks
To Jackie and Mike Campbell, C. J. and Debbie Potter, and the young
people in the Teen Life youth group at Saint Bridget's in Rochester,
New York, for playing along in the development of this material.

To Mary, Chris, David, and Rachel Theisen for being the source of
inspiration that keeps me going and going and going.

GAME SHOW LISTINGS

INTRODUCTION:
TRUTH OR CONSEQUENCES

Hi, we are your Ready-to-Go hosts, Abe and Sarah! We congratulate you on choosing the fun and popular game ideas in this book to help your youth increase their biblical knowledge. And what better way to show you how to use these games than by having you participate in a game yourself. As you answer the following questions, you will be given incredible insights into using this book to achieve maximum learning potential (MLP) with the young people you lead. All you need is 10 minutes of uninterrupted time, a highlighter (optional—and only if you are really into this), and a sense of humor (absolutely essential). So place yourself in a comfortable chair, turn off the phone, and let the game begin!

$1,000 Question: A stitch in time saves what?

   A. the whales
   B. seventy times seven times
   C. your pants from falling down
   D. you from repeating the same thing over and over and over again
   Best response. D

Ever tried to teach someone something that you thought was really cool and they thought NOT? So what did you do? If you are like most of us, you said the same thing again and again, only *louder* so that they and the neighbors could hear you. Sometimes it's not the subject matter that fails us; rather, it is the way we are presenting it.

You already know that first impressions count for a lot. By using formats similar to popular games that are already familiar to most young people, *Ready-to-Go Game Shows* creates an interactive and attention-grabbing environment that makes a great first impression. Once you have the young people's attention, half your job of teaching (usually the most difficult half) is already accomplished!

Ready-to-Go Game Shows was created so that all the shows can be done easily, with minimal setup and few required materials. They really are *ready-to-go*. All you need to do is add young people, mix, and bake with high energy, and you'll get a treat that is really something to talk about. Best of all, each show has been field-tested with both younger and older adolescents who are still alive to talk about it. If at any point you are not 100 percent satisfied with this book, then you can place it in a dark corner of your bookcase where it will make you appear to be an avid reader of interesting books with weird titles.

$10,000 Question: If you had to choose one item to take from your house before it burnt to the ground, which would you most likely select?

    A. your CD collection
    B. your jewelry collection
    C. your computer
    D. your Ready-to-Go supply box (and this book)
    Best response. D

Most of that other stuff can be replaced, but once you put together your game show supply box, you'll really believe it is the most valuable thing in the world (well, close to it anyway). After you gather the suggested items, doing any of the game shows described in this book will be 78 percent easier, leaving a mere 22 percent of the work required to achieve 100 percent MLP.

Suggested items for your Ready-to-Go supply box are these:

- a box (This is always a good place to start.)
- markers
- blank paper
- pen or pencils
- a die (Two dice if you are feeling really lucky!)
- tape (masking and clear)
- two or more Bibles
- prizes (Prizes can be a collection of small items such as pencils—new or already chewed on—fast-food coupons and toys, inspirational bookmarks, leftover Halloween candy with the wrappers intact, new or slightly used toy cars, and so on.)

Once you have your box all put together, keep it away from open flames and in a clean, dry place. Be sure to write in big capital letters somewhere on the box, "MY BOX." This will help deter others from thinking that it is "THEIR BOX," thereby leaving you worry free and once again *ready-to-go.*

An Important Note About the Prize Thing

Achieving MLP is easier if these game shows are more fun than competitive. Whether the game shows are considered pure fun or do-or-die competition is under the direct control of the game show host. So, you might want to make sure that everyone wins a prize or that prizes are given out at random and are all of similar cost. That might mean that absolutely no prizes are awarded to anyone unless they clean up the room when the session is done. Be prepared for arguments and possible hard feelings if you decide to make these game shows more competitive than cooperative.

$100,000 Question: What happened on 31 September 1943 that changed the world?

   A. the Pentateuch was built in Washington, D.C.

   B. the historical books of the old Testament made the *Times* best-
seller list

   C. Matthew, Mark, Luke, and John first appeared on the *Ed
Sullivan Show*

   D. nothing much ever happens on 31 September

Best response. D

To make these game shows learning experiences, the leader must
remember that the questions (and answers) serve as only the beginning
of the learning experience. For example, in answering this question,
some of you may have gone to the Internet to look up the date to see
what *really* happened on 31 September 1943. Others may have already
concluded that nothing happened because 31 September does not
exist. If you had been playing this game show as part of a group, I
would have instructed the group members to turn to their calendars to
find the correct answer, leading the group to ask the obvious question,
"Who hid 31 September and why?"

     These game shows can be used to review biblical material already
covered in your school or parish programs, to introduce new material,
or to entertain an entire school when the special speaker does not
show up for the scheduled assembly. Many of the game show questions
offer *tidbits*, that is, little bits of tid (terrific information drops). The
host can use the tidbits to help the young people to learn more about
the question's topic. These tidbits also help wow the assembled audience by making it appear that the host knows just about everything
there is to know about the Scriptures—which is not a bad thing until
you become a contestant yourself.

     Another way to use the questions as a learning experience is to
have the contestants, teams, or audience look up the scriptural citation
that is supplied with many of the answers. This can lead to a brief

discussion about the person or event that the question refers to. Of course, the longer a particular discussion takes place without the benefit of food, humor, or a bad joke, the more chance you have of losing your audience's attention. Therefore the follow-up should be kept to a minimum unless the group is contained in a high-security area that is well guarded, giving them little or no chance of escape.

$1,000,000 Question: Who was the greatest baby-sitter in the Bible?

    A. Eve
    B. Sarah
    C. Larry the Cucumber
    D. David
    Best response. D (David rocked Goliath to sleep.)

To create MLP, the host needs to be more than a baby-sitter. You will need to take the risk of going beyond the directions and questions in this book and make adaptations to fit the particular needs of your group. Please allow yourself maximum flexibility with each show so that it becomes your show. If you have fun *leading* it, then chances are the young people will have fun *learning* it. Here are five hot suggestions for adapting these game shows.

Start Where the Contestant Is

Try rewording questions (and sometimes even answers) to make them either easier or more challenging for your audience as the need and knowledge level demands it. For example, if the contestant is asked to name the twelve Apostles, you could make it easier by having the contestant name four, six, or eight of the Apostles. Or you could make it harder by asking the contestant to name the twelve Apostles in 30, 45, or 60 seconds. To make it impossible, ask the contestant to name the social security numbers for the Apostles . . . in order from the lowest to the highest.

Choose the Game that Fits Your Group

Some of the game shows are easier than others. Use the game shows that best match the knowledge level of the group you are working with. The easier game shows to play are
- Scriptionary
- The Real Fortune

The games that are of medium difficulty are
- Who Wants to Be a Bible Millionaire
- Faithful Feud
- Holy Word Squares

The game shows that are a bit more challenging are
- Bible Baseball
- The Bible is Right
- Bible Jeopardy

Turn Young People into Scripture Scholars

After playing a particular game and getting a feel for the way the questions are worded, invite the young people to develop their own Bible questions and answers on index cards. Keep the questions in your coveted Ready-to-Go supply box and use them the next time you play the game. The more often you play the games, the better chance you have for achieving MLP.

Bridge the Generation Gap

Use the game shows as a strategy for bringing parents and young people together for an intergenerational event. Pair up parents and young people so that they have to work together as contestants. It may inspire them to read the Bible more at home. Or it might just encourage them to watch reruns of television game shows to learn winning strategies for the next time they play.

$5,000,000 Question: If your best friend jumped into a swimming pool filled with a mixture of six-week-old sour milk and rotten eggs, would you do it too?

A. Yes; after all, it is my best friend.
B. It would depend on what I had just eaten.
C. It would depend on what my best friend had just eaten.
D. No. (My mother always warned me this could happen.)
Best response. D (You are probably seeing the pattern now, right?)

That's right, some things you just have to say no to. In fact, you might as well start to practice saying it: "No!" Try it again: "NO!" You may at times even have to expand on your new word with a phrase such as "No, not now." Or try it in another language, like, "Nada" or "Nyet." Face it, once you start using *Ready-to-Go Game Shows,* you are going to have to tell the young people that there is much more to life than playing games all day long.

This may require you to train a replacement host or at least a cohost or two, who can take over the reins when you are feeling overwhelmed with your string of successful sessions using the game show approach. When you hit this "problem" (and you *will* hit this problem), why not empower a young person (or two or three) to take over for a while. Your protégés might even learn *more* by leading a show than by playing it. Then you will have gone from host extraordinaire to pure MLP genius!

Our Sponsors

Questions and answers for the game shows in this book were created using the following resources:

Klein, Peter. *The Catholic Sourcebook.* Dubuque, IA: Brown-Roa, 2000.
Koch, Carl. *Teaching Manual for Written on Our Hearts: The Old Testament Story of God's Love.* Winona, MN: Saint Mary's Press, 1999.
McKenzie, John L. *Dictionary of the Bible.* New York: Simon and Schuster, 1965.

Singer-Towns, Brian, ed. *The Catholic Youth Bible.* Winona, MN: Saint
   Mary's Press, 2000.
Taylor, Mark D. *The Complete Book of Bible Literacy.* Wheaton, IL:
   Tyndale House, 1992.
Zanzig, Thomas. *Teaching Manual for Jesus of History, Christ of Faith.*
   Winona, MN: Saint Mary's Press, 1999.

A Final Word

If you are still reading this introduction, then you have gone way too
far. Please stop immediately and get started playing some games. After
all, they are all set and *ready-to-go!*

WHO WANTS TO BE
A BIBLE MILLIONAIRE

IS THAT YOUR FiNal ANSWER?

Object of the Game

This game is modeled after the popular game show *Who Wants to Be a Millionaire.* The entire group is invited to participate in a Fast Thinking preliminary round to decide who the lucky contestant will be to sit in the Sweatin' Shekels seat. The winner of the Fast Thinking round gets to try to answer five questions about the Scriptures in order to win up to one million shekels. Each final-round contestant is afforded one of three possible lifelines that can be used to help answer any one question.

HOW THE GAME IS PLAYED

Players Needed

☐ one host
☐ contestants (which can include the entire group or class)

Supplies

☐ a slip of scrap paper or an index card and a pencil for everyone
☐ a Bible for everyone
☐ responses for the Fast Thinking questions written on newsprint or an overhead for all to see
☐ a watch or clock that counts the seconds
☐ prizes for winners by category (candy, books, religious jewelry, class passes, and so on)

Room Setup

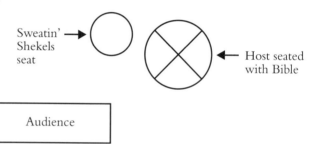

Game Directions

1. The game show host gathers all the contestants around the table, and distributes a pencil and a slip of paper or an index card to all for the Fast Thinking question. The host instructs the contestants to write their name on their paper and the numbers 1 through 4 down the left side of the paper. Then the host tells the group that a question will be read, with four responses listed on the newsprint (or overhead). The contestants must write the responses down in the correct order as

indicated by the question. Only the letter corresponding to each answer needs to be written on the paper.

2. The host reads the Fast Thinking question from the Questions and Answers section that starts on page 21. As soon as the contestants write the letters in the order that they think is correct, they stack their papers beside the Bible on the table. After all the lists are placed next to the Bible, the host turns the pile over and begins checking the lists for accuracy. The first person whose list is correct gets to sit in the Sweatin' Shekels seat for the next series of questions. All the other contestants take a seat in the audience until the round is complete.

3. During the Sweatin' Shekels round, the host asks the player in the Sweatin' Shekels seat up to five questions from the Question and Answer section that starts on page 21, one at a time. The questions become increasingly difficult, and each has four possible answers. When the player is thinking through an answer, the host should ask him or her to do so out loud so that all can hear what's going on in the player's mind. Once the player has selected a final answer, the host asks the audience what they would answer and why. Then the host reveals the correct answer and the tidbit information that is provided.

4. Players can choose one lifeline from the three options listed below, which they may use to help them answer any one of the questions; in other words, they can use only one lifeline once. The host explains these options at the beginning of the game and determines their use during the game. For example, if a player asks for a 50/50, the host determines which two incorrect answers to remove. The lifeline options are these:

- 30-Second Search—The player is given the Bible and 30 seconds to look through it.
- 50/50—The host chooses two answers and deletes them, leaving the correct answer and one incorrect answer for the player to choose from.
- Poll the Audience—The audience uses a show of hands to indicate which answer they think is correct.

Remember, each player gets to use only *one* lifeline during his or her turn in the Sweatin' Shekels seat. As soon as a player misses a question, the game is over for that player and a prize (if any) is awarded. A new round starts with the next Fast Thinking question. Everyone who has not already had a chance in the Sweatin' Shekels seat participates in the new round.

Prizes

Try to secure donations of various prizes from area businesses that are frequented by young people (such as fast-food restaurants, record stores, amusement parks, bowling alleys, and dollar stores) or use various amounts of candy as prizes. Separate the prizes into five categories: 100-, 1,000-, 10,000-, 100,000- and 1,000,000-shekel prizes. For example, using a bag of miniature Tootsie Rolls as prizes, players get one Tootsie Roll if they answer the 100-shekel question correctly, three Tootsie Rolls if they make it to the 1,000-shekel question, and five Tootsie Rolls if they make it to the 10,000-shekel question.

Variations on the Show

Team play. Another way to play this game is to divide the group into teams, and have each team develop five questions and possible answers (from easy to difficult) for the other team or teams and then take turns hosting a show for the group.

PowerPoint presentation. If you or someone in the group has access to PowerPoint and presentation equipment, use it to present the questions and answers with a professional look.

Youth teaching younger children. Have the group take the show on the road, hosting it for younger children's groups or classes, based on what that group or class is studying at the moment.

BIBLE MILLIONAIRE—QUESTIONS AND ANSWERS

Round One Questions

Fast Thinking question. Put the following books in the order they appear in the New Testament:

A. Revelation   C. First Thessalonians

B. Luke   D. Matthew

Answer. D, B, C, A

100-shekel question. Who defeated Goliath?

A. Conan the Barbarian   C. David

B. John the Baptist   D. an angry tax collector

Answer. C

Tidbit. David's defeat of Goliath led to the defeat of the Philistine army and made David a popular hero with the Israelite army.

1,000-shekel question. The word *Sabbath* means

A. "peace"   C. "a day of rest"

B. "Holy One"   D. "What's up?"

Answer. C

Tidbit. The Sabbath (honored by Christians on Sunday and by Jews from sundown Friday to sundown Saturday) is to be set aside for rest and prayer.

10,000-shekel question. The first Gospel to be written was the Gospel of

A. Matthew   C. Luke

B. Mark   D. John

Answer. B

Tidbit. Mark's Gospel was written between A.D. 65 and 70 by a Gentile Christian, possibly a disciple of Peter's. Mark's audience were non-Jewish Christians who were experiencing persecution because of their belief in Jesus. The Gospel's image of Jesus is of a person who places his complete trust in God and accepts suffering as the cost for following God's will.

100,000-shekel question. This twin was later renamed Israel.

A. Joseph   C. Jacob

B. Cain   D. Esau

Answer. C

Tidbit. Jacob, the younger twin brother of Esau, tricked his way into stealing Esau's birthright (Genesis 25:29–34) as well as his father's blessing (Genesis, chapter 27). Jacob later married Leah and Rachel, who gave birth to twelve sons who became known as the twelve tribes of Israel.

1,000,000-shekel question. The official Roman charge against Jesus was that he had

A. committed blasphemy

B. claimed to be a king

C. incited a revolt among the Jews

D. opposed payment of taxes to the Temple

Answer. C

Tidbit. In Luke 23:1–5, the Jewish leaders bring Jesus to Pilate and accuse Jesus of stirring up the people against paying taxes to the emperor. The Jewish leaders do this because they believe that Jesus was blaspheming God by claiming to be divine and therefore want him to be killed. But the Jews cannot sentence a man to death; only the Roman governor can, which is why the Jewish leaders make up the charge that Jesus is inciting a revolt.

Round Two Questions

Fast Thinking question. List these famous women in the order in which they appear in the Bible.

A. Mary Magdalene   C. Sarah

B. Eve   D. Mary, mother of Jesus

Answer. B, C, D, A

100-shekel question. Who visited Mary with the news that she would bear God's Son, Jesus?

A. Sarah
C. the Avon lady

B. the angel Gabriel
D. a census taker

Answer. B

Tidbit. Mary was visited by the angel Gabriel, as told in Luke 1:26–38.

1,000-shekel question. What did Delilah do to Samson to take away his strength?

A. talked him into fighting an army

B. blinded him

C. made him clean the house

D. cut his hair

Answer. D

Tidbit. Delilah tricked Samson into telling her the secret of his strength, then cut his hair while he was sleeping so that the Philistines could capture him. The Philistines blinded him and forced him into slavery. During a Philistine celebration, Samson asked God for one final burst of strength, with which he pushed down two pillars, causing the house to collapse, killing himself and his enemies.

10,000-shekel question. This was the last Gospel to be written.

A. Matthew
C. John

B. Luke
D. Revelation

Answer. C

Tidbit. John's Gospel was written between A.D. 90 and 100 by a member of a Christian community that was founded by the Beloved Disciple. It was written to Christians who were being persecuted by the Romans and thrown out of the Jewish synagogues by the Jews. John's Gospel is quite different from the other three—Matthew, Mark, and Luke—in that it uses a lot of symbolic and poetic language to create a noble, powerful, and divine image of Jesus.

100,000-shekel question. What city was considered King David's place of origin?

    A. Jerusalem   C. Bethlehem

    B. Hebron   D. Nazareth

Answer. C

Tidbit. David, Israel's greatest king, came from the small town of Bethlehem, the same town in which Jesus was born. Sharing a common birthplace connects the greatest king of the Old Testament with Jesus, the new head of the Reign of God.

1,000,000-shekel question. What is the name of Moses' sister?

    A. Deborah   C. Miriam

    B. Zipporah   D. Leah

Answer. C

Tidbit. Immediately after crossing the Red Sea and escaping Pharaoh's grasp, Miriam and Moses sang a canticle rejoicing in their victory over the mighty Egyptians (Exodus 15:1–20). Many consider it to be perhaps the oldest writing in the Bible.

Round Three Questions

Fast Thinking question. Place these commandments in the order in which they appear in the Ten Commandments:

    A. Honor your father and mother.

    B. You shall not steal.

    C. I am the Lord your God . . . you shall have no other gods before me.

    D. Remember the Sabbath day and keep it holy.

Answer. C, D, A, B

100-shekel question. The Gospels tell the story of what?

    A. the life, death, and Resurrection of Jesus

    B. the patriarchs

    C. how the West was won

    D. why the chicken crossed the road

Answer. A

Tidbit. The Gospels—Matthew, Mark, Luke, and John—were written between A.D. 65 and 100 to tell future generations the story of Jesus.

1,000-shekel question. Jesus used these kinds of stories to help people understand what the Reign of God was like.

    A. bedtime stories   C. parables

    B. campfire stories   D. skits

Answer. C

Tidbit. Parables are stories about familiar situations with an unexpected twist (such as the joyful and forgiving father in the parable of the prodigal son or the Samaritan as the hero in the parable of the good Samaritan). These twists allowed people to grasp the radical and inclusive nature of God and God's Reign.

10,000-shekel question. Which king was responsible for building the Jerusalem Temple?

    A. Saul   C. Solomon

    B. David   D. Rehoboam

Answer. C

Tidbit. Solomon, known as the Wise King, designed the Jerusalem Temple after Canaanite models. Completion of the Temple required high taxes and forced labor. The Temple was destroyed in 587 B.C., during the Babylonian invasion.

100,000-shekel question. The term *Passover* is rooted in which event?

    A. the Last Supper   C. the Babylonian Exile

    B. the final plague   D. the Transfiguration

Answer. B

Tidbit. The Passover celebrates the angel of death's passing over all houses marked with lamb's blood during the tenth and final plague brought on Pharaoh and Egypt. The final plague caused Pharaoh to let the Hebrew slaves, led by Moses, go free.

1,000,000-shekel question. Who led the Israelites into the Promised Land of Canaan?

    A. Jacob   C. Aaron

    B. Moses   D. Joshua

Answer. D

Tidbit. Joshua was appointed as Moses' successor (Deuteronomy 31:1–8; Numbers 27:12–23). After Moses' death on Mount Nebo, which overlooks Canaan, Joshua led the Israelites across the Jordan River into the Promised Land of Canaan (Book of Joshua).

Round Four Questions

Fast Thinking question. List these New Testament characters in the order in which they encounter Jesus in the Gospels

    A. Pontius Pilate   C. Simon Peter

    B. John the Baptist   D. Joseph, husband of Mary

Answer. D, B, C, A

100-shekel question. Who led the Hebrews from slavery in Egypt across the Red Sea and to the Promised Land of Canaan?

    A. King David   C. Noah, in his ark

    B. Moses   D. George Washington

Answer. B

Tidbit. Moses, called and guided by God, led the Hebrews from slavery to the Promised Land of Canaan.

1,000-shekel question. Which of these foods did the Israelites depend on as they journeyed in the wilderness with Moses?

    A. Big Macs   C. manna

    B. turkey   D. meatballs

Answer. C

Tidbit. In Exodus 16:4, God promises to feed the hungry Israelites by offering them "bread from heaven," which they find on the ground each morning.

10,000-shekel question. Which of these books is *not* one of the prophetic books of the Old Testament?

    A. Jeremiah   C. Isaiah

    B. Leviticus   D. Daniel

Answer. B

Tidbit. Leviticus is part of the Pentateuch, or the first five books of the Bible (referred to as the Torah by the Jews). There are eighteen prophetic books, each divided into major and minor prophets.

100,000-shekel question. The Sermon on the Mount, in which Jesus teaches the Beatitudes, can be found in which Gospel?

    A. Matthew   C. Luke

    B. Mark   D. John

Answer. A

Tidbit. The Sermon on the Mount is found in Matthew, chapter 5, and is an outline of the challenging lifestyle that the Reign of God demands. Although Luke also contains the Beatitudes (6:17–26), it says that they were taught on a plain, not on a mountain.

1,000,000-shekel question. Pentecost commemorates what event for the Jews?

    A. the Exodus from Egypt

    B. the giving of the Law to Moses

    C. the fall of Jericho

    D. the Holy Spirit's inspiring the Apostles

Answer. B

Tidbit. Pentecost is an annual celebration by Jews of the giving of the Law (summarized in the Ten Commandments) to Moses. It is celebrated fifty days after the feast of Passover by Jews, and on the seventh Sunday after Easter by Christians. During the first Pentecost, after the Resurrection of Jesus, the Apostles were filled with the Holy Spirit and began to preach the Good News of Jesus Christ, giving the feast a new meaning for Christians.

Round Five Questions

Fast Thinking question. List these famous leaders in the order in which they appear in the Old Testament.

A. Jacob   C. Moses

B. Abraham   D. Isaac

Answer. B, D, A, C

100-shekel question. Who is often credited with writing many of the Psalms?

A. The Grateful Dead   C. King David

B. King Elvis   D. The Rolling Stones

Answer. C

Tidbit. David is often credited with writing the Psalms, probably because he was known to enjoy writing and performing music, but it is believed that most of the Psalms were written long after David's death.

1,000-shekel question. Who wrote the Letter to the Romans?

A. Peter   C. Mary

B. Paul   D. John

Answer. B

Tidbit. Paul wrote the Letter to the Romans around A.D. 56 to Jewish and Gentile Christians living in Rome. He is credited with writing many of the epistles.

10,000-shekel question. In which Gospel does Jesus wash the disciples' feet during the Last Supper?

A. Matthew   C. Luke

B. Mark   D. John

Answer. D

Tidbit. In John, chapter 13, Jesus washes the disciples' feet to make the point that serving others is at the heart of being a follower of Jesus. We celebrate this message every Holy Thursday during the Easter Triduum (the three days beginning with Holy Thursday and ending with Easter, during Holy Week).

100,000-shekel question. The Acts of the Apostles was written by

    A. John   C. Paul

    B. Luke   D. Peter

Answer. B

Tidbit. The Gospel of Luke and the Acts of the Apostles were written as a two-volume set (around A.D. 80) but were split up when the Bible was put together. The Acts of the Apostles tells the story of the early church from Pentecost until Paul takes Christianity to Rome, then the center of the known world.

1,000,000-shekel question. Who claimed Jesus' body after the Crucifixion?

    A. Mary Magdelene   C. Nicodemus

    B. John, the Beloved Disciple D. Joseph of Arimathea

Answer. D

Tidbit. Joseph of Arimathea was a member of the Sanhedrin (Jewish council) and a disciple of Jesus', who obtained the body of Jesus and buried it in his family tomb.

Round Six Questions

Fast Thinking question. List these major sections of the Bible in the order in which they appear.

    A. the historical books   C. the Pentateuch

    B. the Gospels   D. the epistles

Answer. C, A, B, D

100-shekel question. To test Abraham's faith, God instructed him to sacrifice his only what?

    A. walking stick   C. pillow

    B. chicken   D. son, Isaac

Answer. D

Tidbit. God asked Abraham to sacrifice Isaac, his and Sarah's only son, but sent a messenger to stop Abraham at the last minute.

1,000-shekel question. The ark of the Covenant contained what?

    A. the Ten Commandments

    B. used oil lamps

    C. the remains of Moses

    D. Noah and a whole lot of animals

Answer. A

Tidbit. The ark of the Covenant contained the two stone tablets on which the Mosaic law (Ten Commandments) was written. It was paraded in front of the Israelite army before battle to ensure victory.

10,000-shekel question. The most important and powerful person in the Jewish community during the time of Jesus was the

A. Pharisee	C. tax collector
B. high priest	D. scribe

Answer. B

Tidbit. The high priest served as the president of the Sanhedrin and the chief representative of the people to the ruling power (Rome). He was the only one who entered the holy of holies (the innermost and most sacred chamber of the Temple) to purify it on the Day of Atonement.

100,000-shekel question. Who was the emperor of Rome at the time of Jesus' birth?

A. Nero	C. Caesar Augustus
B. Herod	D. Pontius Pilate

Answer. C

Tidbit. Caesar Augustus ordered the census that led Mary and Joseph to Bethlehem (Matthew, chapter 2).

1,000,000-shekel question. Who created the golden calf for the Israelites while they were waiting for Moses to return from Mount Sinai?

A. Aaron	C. Ahab
B. Joshua	D. Joash

Answer. A

Tidbit. Aaron, the brother of Moses, created the golden calf while Moses was on Mount Sinai receiving the Ten Commandments (Exodus, chapter 32). Upon seeing the calf, Moses threw the stone tablets down at Aaron's feet in a fit of rage, breaking the tablets into pieces.

Round Seven Questions

Fast Thinking question. List these major biblical events in the order in which they appear in the Scriptures, starting with the most recent.

     A. Moses is called.

     B. Jesus walks on water.

     C. Mary says yes to the angel Gabriel.

     D. David is crowned king of Israel.

Answer. B, C, D, A

100-shekel question. What is the correct ending to the verse "Blessed are the poor in spirit . . ."?

     A. for they will receive an allowance

     B. for they should get a job

     C. for theirs is the kingdom of heaven

     D. Is that your final answer?

Answer. C

Tidbit. This is the first line of the Beatitudes, found in Matthew, chapter 5, outlining the radical nature of the Reign of God.

1,000-shekel question. The mother of John the Baptist was

     A. Maude   C. Eve

     B. Miriam   D. Elizabeth

Answer. D

Tidbit. Elizabeth was Mary's older cousin, whom she visited soon after being visited by the angel Gabriel. When John was born, his father, Zechariah, proclaimed a song called the Canticle of Zechariah.

10,000-shekel question. After spending forty days in the desert, from what prophetic scroll did Jesus read while he was in the synagogue in Nazareth?

    A. Isaiah   C. Daniel

    B. Jeremiah   D. Ezekiel

Answer. A

Tidbit. In Luke 4:16–30, Jesus arrives in Nazareth, his hometown, and reads the section from Isaiah that begins "The Spirit of the Lord is upon me, because he has anointed me." Upon completing the reading, Jesus announces that the Scriptures have now been fulfilled.

100,000-shekel question. What did God ask Hosea the prophet to do?

    A. interpret the dreams of King Nebuchadnezzar

    B. marry a prostitute

    C. circle Ephraim seven times, calling it to repentance

    D. spend the night in a lion's den

Answer. B

Tidbit. God told Hosea to marry Gomer, a prostitute who continued to be unfaithful to Hosea. However, Hosea remained faithful to and forgiving of Gomer as a sign of how God would remain faithful to and forgiving of the Hebrew people, even when they drifted away from their Covenant with God.

1,000,000-shekel question. Which nation overthrew the Northern Kingdom of Israel in 722 B.C.?

    A. Assyria   C. Rome

    B. Babylon   D. Philistia

Answer. A

Tidbit. The Assyrians captured Samaria in 721 B.C., ending the nation of Israel (known as the Northern Kingdom). Judah (known as the Southern Kingdom) would fall to the Babylonians in 587 B.C.

Round Eight Questions

Fast Thinking question. List these events in the life of Jesus in the order in which they occurred.

    A. Jesus invites Thomas to probe the nail marks in his hands and feet.

    B. Judas betrays Jesus with a kiss.

    C. Jesus is baptized in the Jordan River by John.

    D. Jesus raises Lazarus from the dead.

Answer. C, D, B, A

100-shekel question. The word *genesis* means

    A. "beginning"   C. "Gene's sister"

    B. "ending"   D. "Gene's mother"

Answer. A

Tidbit. Genesis is the first book of the Bible. It contains the Creation stories and the stories of the patriarchs and their relationships and offspring.

1,000-shekel question. *Shalom* means

    A. "May I take your order?"

    B. "You the man!"

    C. "a deep peace"

    D. "a time for forgiveness and debt reduction"

Answer. C

Tidbit. "Shalom" is a customary greeting and farewell used by Jews to wish others a sense of peace that is rooted in God.

10,000-shekel question. In the Book of Numbers, who challenges Moses' authority?

    A. Jacob   C. Levi

    B. Joshua and Anna   D. Miriam and Aaron

Answer. D

Tidbit. In Numbers, chapter 12, Miriam and Aaron, Moses' siblings, speak against Moses for marrying a Cushite woman. God curses Miriam for doing so by making her leprous for seven days.

100,000-shekel question. What makes Deborah a unique biblical figure?

    A. She was the mother of Gideon.

    B. She helped Samson escape from the Philistines.

    C. She was one of Israel's judges, and she led an army.

    D. She hid Joshua from his enemies while he spied in Jericho.

Answer. C

Tidbit. In Judges, chapters 4–5, we see how Deborah, a female judge, or "deliverer," for Israel, teams up with Barak to defeat Sisera, a Canaanite general. Afterward, she sings the Song of Deborah (chapter 5), regarded as one of the oldest texts in the Bible.

1,000,000-shekel question. Whose hands restored Saul's sight after he was blinded on the road to Damascus?

    A. Ananias'   C. Barnabas'

    B. Peter's   D. Cornelius'

Answer. A

Tidbit. Ananias was a Christian leader who was prompted by God to lay hands on Saul to restore his sight (Acts of the Apostles, chapter 9). After that experience, Saul converted to Christianity and became Paul, the greatest missionary of the early church.

Round Nine Questions

Fast Thinking question. List these events in the life of Moses in the order in which they happened.

    A. Moses announces the ten plagues on Egypt.

    B. Moses is found in the Nile.

    C. Moses leads the Hebrews across the Red Sea.

    D. Moses meets God in the burning bush.

Answer. B, D, A, C

100-shekel question. Which of these was *not* an Apostle of Jesus?

    A. Peter   C. John

    B. James   D. Lancelot

Answer. D

Tidbit. Peter, James, and John are often portrayed as Jesus' closest disciples. For example, they are the only Apostles who witnessed the Transfiguration (Matthew 17:1–7, Mark 9:2–13, Luke 9:28–36).

1,000-shekel question. What did Joseph receive from his father, Jacob, as a sign of special favor that made his eleven brothers jealous?

    A. a goat

    B. a new chariot with air-conditioning

    C. a new tent

    D. a coat of many colors

Answer. D

Tidbit. The story of Joseph and his brothers is told in the popular musical *Joseph and the Amazing Technicolor Dreamcoat.* The multi-colored coat is actually referred to as "the long robe with sleeves" in many biblical accounts (for example, Genesis 37:3). Joseph was the favored son of Jacob and Rachel. After being sold into slavery by his brothers, he rose to power in Egypt due to his ability to interpret dreams.

10,000-shekel question. According to the Gospel of John, what was Jesus' first miracle?

    A. healing a paralytic

    B. turning water into wine

    C. walking on water

    D. restoring sight to the blind Bartimaeus

Answer. B

Tidbit. At a wedding feast in Cana, Jesus changed water into wine at the urging of his mother, Mary (John, chapter 2).

100,00-shekel question. Before his conversion to Christianity, Paul was a

A. farmer   C. tax collector

B. Pharisee   D. soldier

Answer. B

Tidbit. The Pharisees were Jews who believed that salvation was achieved by rigorously following the Jewish Law. Paul was a rigid Pharisee who made a living as a tent maker and who persecuted the early Christians until his own conversion to faith in Christ.

1,000,000-shekel question. Who was Hannah and Elkanah's first-born son?

A. David   C. Samuel

B. Joshua   D. Eli

Answer. C

Tidbit. Hannah's humble prayer to God for a child (1 Samuel, chapters 1–2) resulted in her giving birth to Samuel, the last of the judges and the prophet who anointed the first king of Israel, Saul.

Round Ten Questions

Fast Thinking question. List these Gospels in the order in which they appear in the Bible, *from last to first.*

A. Mark   C. Matthew

B. John   D. Luke

Answer. B, D, A, C

100-shekel question. Before the Israelites stormed Jericho, they

    A. danced the Macarena

    B. sang a rousing version of "And the Walls Came Tumblin' Down"

    C. circled the city seven times blowing rams' horns

    D. gave a Bronx cheer

Answer. C

Tidbit. The taking of Jericho fulfilled God's Promise to the Israelites that they would live in Canaan. The story is told in Joshua, Chapter 6.

1,000-shekel question. Why did Sarah laugh when three men told her that she and Abraham would have a son?

    A. They already had twenty children.

    B. The men were sitting in a pile of old sheep droppings.

    C. Abraham and Sarah were not even married yet.

    D. Sarah was very old.

Answer. D

Tidbit. God promised Abraham and Sarah that they would be the parents of a multitude of nations and that their descendants would be as numerous as the stars of heaven (Genesis 22:17). They were visited by three strangers who announced that Sarah would give birth to a son, and Sarah laughed because she was very old (Genesis, chapter 18). Later, she gave birth to Isaac.

10,000-shekel question. The official governing body of the Jews during Jesus' time was the

    A. Sanhedrin   C. Temple scribe

    B. high priest   D. Shema

Answer. A

Tidbit. The Sanhedrin was composed of priests, Pharisees, and scribes, with the high priest serving as president. It had a good deal of civil authority under the rule of the Romans, but it did not have the authority to give the death sentence, which is why it had to send Jesus to Herod and Pilate to be sentenced to death.

100,000-shekel question. The priests in ancient Israel were members of this tribe.

A. Benjamin's   C. Levi's

B. Dan's   D. Judah's

Answer. C

Tidbit. Levi was one of Jacob's twelve sons (who became the twelve tribes of Israel). The Levites (descendants of Levi) became the priests and temple workers and were supported by the other tribes through tithes.

1,000,000-shekel question. Who was Paul's first convert in the region of Philippi?

A. Silas   C. Simeon

B. Priscilla   D. Lydia

Answer. D

Tidbit. In Acts of the Apostles 16:11–15, we find the story of Lydia's conversion. Lydia is a textile merchant and wealthy enough to support her household and to invite Paul and Silas to stay at her home during their missionary work in Philippi.

FAITHFUL FEUD

Object of the Game

Modeled after the game show *Family Feud*, this game invites teams of contestants to guess all the responses to fictitious biblical surveys about scriptural events and people before they get three strikes, or misses. The opposing team may steal all the points if they correctly guess the survey responses that have not already been revealed.

HOW THE GAME IS PLAYED

Players Needed

- ☐ one host
- ☐ two or more teams of four contestants
- ☐ one scribe (scorekeeper)

Supplies

- ☐ two sets of survey questions and responses (one for the host and one for the scorekeeper)
- ☐ an answer board (see setup below) using a chalkboard and chalk, an overhead projector, or newsprint and marker
- ☐ small prizes (optional)
- ☐ a Bible for everyone (optional)

Room Setup

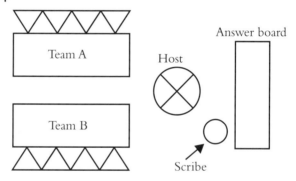

Answer Board Setup

Rank Response	Rank Response	Team Score	
		A	B
1.	6.		
2.	7.		
3.	8.		
4.	9.	Strikes	
5.	10.	☐ ☐ ☐	

Game Directions

1. The host divides the group into teams of four people. If there are more than two teams, the host chooses two to play the game and the rest are seated as the audience. The host identifies one of the playing teams as team A, and the other as team B.

2. The host invites one person from each playing team to step forward to compete in a toss-up question.

3. For the toss-up question, the host reads one of the survey questions from pages 46–51. The first player to yell "BEEP!" responds with a word or phrase that he or she thinks is one of the survey responses. If the player's response matches one of the responses given for that question, the scribe writes the word or phrase on the appropriate numbered line on the answer board and notes the appropriate points from the scoring chart on page 42. If it is not the top answer, the opposing player has the opportunity to guess a higher-ranked response. The team of the player who guesses the highest-ranked response has the option to pass or play.

4. If a team passes, the opposing team must try to guess all the correct responses to the toss-up question. If a team plays, they must try to guess all the responses themselves.

5. The host then invites the next person on the playing team to guess another response. No one is allowed to assist the person who is guessing. If someone does try to assist, the team receives a strike.

6. If the response the second person gives is listed on pages 46–51, the scribe writes it in the correct space on the answer board. If the response is not one of the listed survey responses, the scribe records a strike (an X) on the answer board.

7. Play then goes to the next person on the team. This process is repeated until the team gets three strikes or correctly guesses all ten responses. If the team guesses all ten responses, they receive the maximum total of 55 points and the round is over.

8. If the team gets three strikes before guessing all the responses, the opposing team has the option of stealing the points earned so far. The opposing team gets one guess at another correct response. The team members may confer with one another to determine the best

guess. If their answer is on the list, the team receives the total points earned by the other team, and the round is over. If the team's response is not on the list, the first team keeps their points and the round is over.

9. Once a round is completed, each team sends a new person forward to answer the toss-up question for the next round, and the game continues as before.

10. The game continues for a set number of rounds or a set time. Three rounds or 15 minutes makes a good game, especially if several teams play. The team with the highest score when time is called is declared the "Faithful Feud" winner and may be awarded prizes. When the game is finished, the host invites two new teams to play.

Scoring Chart

Each correct answer receives a score from 1 to 10, as follows:

Survey Answer Rank	Points
1	10
2	9
3	8
4	7
5	6
6	5
7	4
8	3
9	2
10	1

Example: If all responses were guessed, a maximum score of 55 would be awarded.

Host Instructions

1. Recruit a scribe ahead of time, and review with that person the process of scoring and giving strikes for incorrect answers. Practice a round with the scribe if necessary so that he or she is not confused what to do during the actual game.

2. The survey questions have been written in such a way that you can ask them with a humorous or exaggerated emphasis. The actual responses are not the result of any scientific survey, so feel free to embellish the "authenticity" of the survey as much as you wish.

3. Consider beginning the game by reading the optional introductory script on pages 44–45. Then call forward your first two players and have them stand facing you. Tell them that as soon as they think they know a correct survey response they should shout out "Beep!" and immediately offer their response.

4. When time is up, declare the winning team and award prizes (optional).

Variations on the Show

Involve everyone. There are several ways to involve everyone in this game:

- If your group is small enough, adjust the size of the teams to include everyone. Let the teams discuss possible answers and respond through one player designated as their captain. After three strikes, send the play to the opposite team for their one chance at "stealing" by offering a correct answer.
- Divide the group into sets of teams (red team A and B, blue team A and B, and so on) and alternate teams after each round (for example, blue team B switches with blue team A after round 1).

Audience participation. After the teams have finished guessing and before any remaining survey responses are revealed, allow the audience to guess the remaining correct responses. Award small candy prizes for guessing a correct answer.

Real family feud. Use this as an intergenerational event with families and extended families competing against one another like they do on the *Family Feud* show.

INTRODUCTORY SCRIPT

To help keep the fun of this game in perspective, consider having the host use the following script to get the show—and the humor—going.

Hello, and welcome to your favorite Scripture game show, "Faithful Feud!" This is the show where teams get to argue about the answers to incredibly scientific surveys that have taken thousands of years to make up. The game is simple. We surveyed numerous people and animals over the years that the Bible was being written and compiled, and put together surveys that seek the top ten answers to the questions they ask.

That's where you, our highly competitive teams, come in. Each team will have the opportunity to test its biblical knowledge and abilities by offering responses to these surveys, *when it is your turn* (and it's not your turn, so be quiet, please!).

One person from each team will be invited to come forward and stand next to me. I will ask a toss-up question. As soon as you think you know a correct response, you should toss up your hand (nothing else, please) and say **"BEEP!"** Why don't we practice that now, ready . . . **go!**

Wonderful, I'm having fun already, aren't you?! Anyway, the first person to say "BEEP!" must offer a response immediately. If the response is on the survey, then our highly paid scribe will indicate what ranking and score it gets. If it is not the number 1 ranking, then the opposing player gets one guess to try and top it. The player with the highest-ranked response gets to decide whether his or her team will pass (to the other team) or play the round themselves.

The team playing the round will take turns guessing a response. When you are correct, you'll hear this: "You're correct." If you are wrong, you will hear this: "   ." That was the sound of *nothing.* And while you are listening to that sound, you will see our highly paid scribe place an *X* on the board. Get three *X*s, and the other team gets a chance to *steal* the win by guessing one of the remaining responses with one try. If they correctly guess any of the remaining responses, they will be thought of as pretty smart! Not only that, but they will win all the points that have been amassed by your team (which is pretty unfair, if you ask me). However, if their one guess is not on the survey, your team receives the point total, and all is well in the world again.

The winning team will be the one with the most points when time expires or when I expire, whichever comes first.

Now that you are totally confused, are you ready to be faithful? Then let's play **"Faithful Feud!!!"**

FAITHFUL FEUD—SURVEY QUESTIONS AND RESPONSES

I. A group of about five thousand men, women, and children sitting on a hillside in Galilee were asked, "What is your favorite parable told by Jesus?"

Rank   *Answer*
1.   The good Samaritan (Luke 10:30–37)
2.   The prodigal son (Luke 15:11–32)
3.   The sower and the seed (Matthew 13:3–8,18–23; Mark 4:3–9,14–20; Luke 8:5–15)
4.   The lost sheep (Matthew 18:12–14, Luke 15:3–7)
5.   The mustard seed (Matthew 13:31–32, Mark 4:30–32, Luke 13:18–19)
6.   The lamp under a bushel basket (Matthew 5:14–16)
7.   The wedding banquet (Matthew 22:1–14)
8.   The sheep and the goats (Matthew 25:31–46)
9.   The talents (Matthew 25:14–30)
10.   The rich man and Lazarus (Luke 16:19–31)

2. Thousands of Hebrews wandering the desert with Moses (after crossing the Red Sea) were asked to "Name one of the top Ten Commandments of all time."

Rank   *Answer*
1.   I am the Lord your God, you shall have no other gods before me.
2.   You shall not make wrongful use of the name of the Lord your God.
3.   Remember the Sabbath day, and keep it holy.
4.   Honor your father and your mother.
5.   You shall not murder.
6.   You shall not commit adultery.
7.   You shall not steal.

Permission to reproduce this page for program use is granted.

8. You shall not bear false witness against your neighbor.
9. You shall not covet your neighbor's wife.
10. You shall not covet your neighbor's goods.

3. One hundred people who read the Bible were asked, "What woman of the Bible do you admire most?"

Rank   Answer
1. Mary, mother of God (Luke 1:26—2:20)
2. Sarah, wife of Abraham (Genesis 17:15 –16; 21:1–7)
3. Mary Magdalene, follower of Jesus (John 20:1–18)
4. Ruth, wife of Boaz and great-grandmother of King David (Book of Ruth)
5. Eve (Genesis 2:18—3:20)
6. Elizabeth, mother of John the Baptist (Luke 1:5 –25,57– 66)
7. Rebekah, wife of Isaac and mother of Jacob (Genesis, chapter 24)
8. Rachel, wife of the patriarch Jacob and mother of Joseph and Benjamin (Genesis, chapter 29)
9. Hannah, wife of Elkanah and mother of Samuel (1 Samuel 1:1—2:11)
10. Lydia or Priscilla, early disciples with Paul (Acts of the Apostles 16:11–15, chapter 8)

4. Thousands of followers of Jesus were asked, "What was the most amazing miracle you ever saw Jesus do?"

Rank   Answer
1. Walk on water (Matthew 14:22–33, Mark 6:45–52, John 6:16–21)
2. Feed five thousand people (Matthew 14:13–21, Mark 6:30 –34, Luke 9:10 –17, John 6:1–15)
3. Raise Lazarus from the dead (John 11:1– 44)
4. Turn water into wine (John 2:1–11)

5.   Heal the blind (Matthew 9:27–31, 12:22, 20:29–34; Mark 8:22–26, 10:46–52; Luke 18:35–43; John 5:1–9

6.   Calm the storm (Matthew 8:23–27, Mark 4:35–41, Luke 8:22–25)

7.   Heal the paralytic (Matthew 9:1–8, Mark 2:1–12, Luke 5:17–26)

8.   Heal the centurion's servant (Matthew 8:5–13, Luke 7:1–10)

9.   Catch a great amount of fish (Luke 5:1–11, John 21:1–11)

10.   Heal the ten lepers (Luke 17:11–19)

5. A school of fish were asked, "What is your favorite Bible story involving water?"

Rank   *Answer*

1.   Moses parts the Red Sea (Exodus, chapter 14)

2.   The baptism of Jesus in the Jordan River (Matthew 3:13–17, Mark 1:9–11, Luke 3:21–22)

3.   Jonah and the whale (Jonah, chapters 1 and 2)

4.   Jesus turns water into wine (John 2:1–11)

5.   Noah and the Great Flood (Genesis, chapters 6–9)

6.   Jesus walks on water (Matthew 14:22–33, Mark 6:45–52, John 6:16–21)

7.   Jesus calms the storm (Matthew 8:23–27, Mark 4:35–41, Luke 8:22–25)

8.   The Samaritan woman at the well (John 4:1–42)

9.   Moses gets water from a rock (Exodus 17:1–7)

10.   The shipwreck of Paul (Acts of the Apostles, chapter 27)

6. One thousand Hebrews were asked, "Who is the most renowned Old Testament prophet?"

Rank   *Answer*

1.   Moses

2.   Samuel

3. Elijah
4. Isaiah
5. Jeremiah
6. Daniel
7. Hosea
8. Ezekiel
9. Micah
10. Habakkuk

7. Just before crossing the Red Sea, Pharaoh was asked, "What were the worst plagues you ever experienced?"

Rank   Answer (in order of appearance)
1. The water of the Nile turned to blood (Exodus 7:14–25)
2. Frogs covered the land (Exodus 8:1–15)
3. Gnats covered the land (Exodus 8:16–19)
4. Flies covered the land (Exodus 8:20–30)
5. Livestock died of disease (Exodus 9:1–7)
6. People and animals were covered with boils (Exodus 9:8–12)
7. A hailstorm ravaged the land (Exodus 9:13–35)
8. Locusts covered the land (Exodus 10:1–20)
9. Darkness covered the land for three days (Exodus 10:21–29)
10. The firstborn son in every household was killed (Exodus 11:1—12:32)

8. One million tour guides from the Holy Land were asked, "What are the top sites Jesus visited?"

Rank   Answer
1. Jerusalem, where Jesus was crucified and resurrected (Matthew 27:11—28:10, Mark 15:1—16:13, Luke 23:26—24:53, John 19:16—20:29)
2. Jordan River, where Jesus was baptized by John (Matthew 3:13–17)

3.   Capernaum, where Jesus healed the centurion's servant (Matthew 8:5–13, Luke 7:1–10) and a paralytic (Matthew 9:1–8, Mark 2:1–12, Luke 5:17–26) and raised Jairus's daughter (Matthew 9:18–26)

4.   Nazareth, where Jesus grew up (Luke 2:39–40)

5.   Sea of Galilee, where Jesus called the first disciples, calmed the storm (Matthew 8:23–27, Mark 4:35–41, Luke 8:22–25), and walked on the water (Matthew 14:22–33, Mark 6:45–52, John 6:16–21)

6.   Cana, where Jesus performed a miracle at a wedding feast (John 2:1–11)

7.   Samaria, where Jesus talked to a Samaritan woman at the well (John 4:1–42)

8.   Bethlehem, where Jesus was born (Luke 2:1–7)

9.   Jericho, where Jesus healed Bartimaeus (Mark 10:46–52) and called Zacchaeus (Luke 19:1–10)

10. Bethany, where Jesus raised Lazarus (John 11:1–44)

9. Ten thousand religion teachers were asked, "What are the most important names to remember from the Scriptures?"

Rank   Answer
1.   God (Yahweh)
2.   Jesus
3.   Mary, mother of God
4.   Peter
5.   Paul
6.   Moses
7.   David
8.   the patriarchs (Abraham, Isaac, and Jacob)
9.   Solomon
10.   Joseph, Mary's husband

10. Twenty-five hundred Bible readers were asked, "What is your favorite epistle (letter) in the New Testament?"

Rank	Answer
1.	Romans
2.	First or Second Corinthians
3.	First or Second Thessalonians
4.	Galatians
5.	Philippians
6.	Colossians
7.	Ephesians
8.	Hebrews
9.	First or Second Timothy
10.	First, Second, or Third John

BIBLE JEOPARDY

Object of the Game

Modeled after the popular game show *Jeopardy*, this game challenges contestants to attempt to answer questions in different categories that are organized according to biblical themes. The answers must be stated in the form of a question. As the questions get harder, they are worth more points for the person or team that answers them correctly.

HOW THE GAME IS PLAYED

Players Needed

- ☐ one host
- ☐ three contestants or teams
- ☐ one scribe (scorekeeper)

Supplies

- ☐ a game board (see setup on next page), using a chalkboard and chalk, an overhead projector, a whiteboard, or newsprint and markers
- ☐ a clock or watch that counts seconds
- ☐ a Bible for everyone (optional)
- ☐ prizes for the participants (optional)

Room Setup

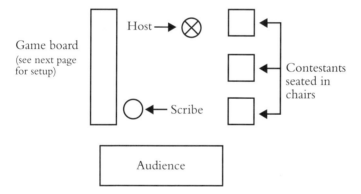

Game Board Setup

Category A	Category B	Category C	Category D
100	100	100	100
200	200	200	200
300	300	300	300
400	400	400	400
500	500	500	500

Score

Contestant 1: _____

Contestant 2: _____

Contestant 3: _____

Game Directions

1. The host selects four categories from those given in "Bible Jeopardy—Answers and Questions," on pages 56–65, and writes each category above the points columns on the game board. Then the host selects three contestants and introduces them to the audience. Each contestant is seated in a chair.

2. The shortest contestant goes first. He or she chooses any category and point amount on the board. The host reads the answer that corresponds to the chosen category and point amount from "Bible Jeopardy—Answers and Questions" (pages 56–65). The contestant has 10 seconds to respond *in the form of a question.*

3. If the contestant responds correctly, the host declares the points won, and the scribe crosses them off the points column and adds them to the contestant's score. Whenever a correct answer is given, the host shares the background tidbit to it, or may encourage the contestants to find the particular response in their Bible.

4. If the response is incorrect or if there is no response within 10 seconds, the question is up for grabs to the other two contestants. As soon

as the host says that a question is up for grabs, the *irst person to stand up* gets to answer it. If the answer is correct, the points are added to the contestant's score; if the answer is incorrect, the points are deducted from the contestant's score, and the remaining contestant has an opportunity to answer the question. If no one gives the correct answer, the host reveals the answer and shares the tidbit, and the scribe crosses the points off the game board.

5.   The game then proceeds with the contestant to the right of the person who had the first chance at the previous question. No one loses a turn when a question goes up for grabs.

6.   The game continues until all the points on the game board have been crossed off or until time expires. The contestant with the most points at the end wins the game. The host announces the winner and awards prizes, if they are being used.

Prizes

Prizes can be awarded to first, second, and third place, or one large prize can be awarded to the winner and two smaller ones to the other contestants. When selecting and awarding prizes, remember that the emphasis is on learning Bible facts and information and having fun, not on competition and prizes.

Variations on the Show

Family play. If you are working with families, select three of them (or three parent-child teams) to play. Select a captain to be the spokesperson for each team.

Group play. Invite everyone in the group to play by having each person select a category and amount and attempt to answer the question. Give each member of the group a turn.

BIBLE JEOPARDY—ANSWERS AND QUESTIONS

Category: Patriarchs and Matriarchs

100 Points. This first patriarch was asked to make quite a sacrifice.

Correct question. Who is Abraham?

Tidbit. God tested Abraham's faith and trust by asking Abraham to offer his only son, Isaac, as a sacrifice, and then sending an angel to stop Abraham just before he could deliver the fatal blow.

200 Points. Long past her childbearing years, she had to laugh when a mysterious guest first announced news of her pregnancy to her and her husband, Abraham.

Correct question. Who is Sarah?

Tidbit. Sarah was an old lady when God blessed her with a son, Isaac.

300 Points. He dreamed too much, so his brothers sold him into slavery and tore up his prized coat, but he ended up living the dream.

Correct question. Who is Joseph?

Tidbit. Joseph was the favorite son of Jacob and Rachel, and his jealous brothers tried to get rid of him. But his brothers ended up bowing to him after he made it big with Pharaoh by interpreting the Pharaoh's dreams and preparing Egypt for a great famine.

400 Points. God promised him that his twelve sons would become the leaders of the twelve tribes of Israel and even changed his name to fit the promise.

Correct question. Who is Jacob?

Tidbit. Jacob was renamed Israel, and his twelve sons led the twelve tribes of Israel.

500 Points. He married Rebekah, and their children developed a clear case of sibling rivalry.

Correct uestion. Who is Isaac?

Tidbit. Isaac and Rebekah gave birth to Esau and Jacob, who fought and competed with each other throughout their lives. Jacob actually stole Esau's birthright and blessing.

Category: Exodus

100 Points. This early leader parted ways with Pharaoh at the Red Sea.

Correct uestion. Who is Moses?

Tidbit. Moses helped the Hebrews through the Exodus experience, leading them from slavery to freedom.

200 Points. Moses was born a Hebrew, but he rode the current into this culture.

Correct uestion. What is the Egyptian culture?

Tidbit. Moses' mother placed him in a basket and sent him down the Nile River, where he was found by Pharaoh's daughter, who raised him as her own.

300 Points. While Moses was off tending his flock, this sight stopped him in his tracks and left him sandleless.

Correct uestion. What is the burning bush?

Tidbit. Moses encountered God on Mount Horeb in the form of a burning bush. That is where God first revealed God's name to humanity by declaring, "I Am Who Am."

400 Points. This commemorates the last and greatest plague on Egypt and a Jewish feast that is still celebrated today.

Correct uestion. What is Passover?

Tidbit. Passover celebrates the night God sent the angel of death to kill the firstborn son of every household except those whose houses were marked with the blood of a lamb. The marked houses were "passed over."

500 Points. This box held a commanding presence wherever it went.

Correct uestion. What is the ark of the Covenant?

Tidbit. This was the sacred box that was specially made to hold the tablets of the Law—the Ten Commandments—and possibly other sacred items that symbolized God's saving presence among the Israelites.

Category: Prophets

100 Points. This prophet told God that he stuttered and was too young to speak. God took care of his difficulties with a soft touch and a few choice words.

Correct uestion. Who was Jeremiah?

Tidbit. Jeremiah was a major prophet who was sent by God to preach a hard message of repentance for Israel's sin and corruption.

200 Points. When God was looking for someone to send, this prophet's response, "Here I Am, Lord," was music to God's ears.

Correct uestion. Who is Isaiah?

Tidbit. Isaiah 6:8 carries this unforgettable response that all prophets—and Christians—are invited to speak.

300 Points. This prophet was not on the lion's menu.

Correct uestion. Who is Daniel?

Tidbit. Daniel was thrown into the lion's den after breaking a law that stated that no one could pray to any god or person other than the king. Daniel survived a night in the lion's den and was released with the king praising his faith and his God.

400 Points. This famous prophet rode first-class to heaven—in a chariot of fire.

Correct Question. Who is Elijah?

Tidbit. Elijah was a passionate prophet who challenged the division of class in Israel and denounced the unfaithfulness of Queen Jezebel and Kings Ahab and Ahaziah. Elijah's dramatic departure is found in Second Kings 2:11–12.

500 Points. After God told him to marry an unfaithful prostitute named Gomer, this prophet never lost faith in God or Gomer.

Correct uestion. Who is Hosea?

Tidbit. God used Hosea's marriage to an unfaithful woman as a symbol of God's unconditional love for the unfaithful Israelites.

Category: Judges and Kings

100 Points. The first king of Israel, he stood head and shoulders above the rest until a small shepherd boy took center stage.

Correct uestion. Who is King Saul?

Tidbit. Saul's story is found in First Samuel, chapters 9–31. Because Saul did not fully obey God, his throne was given to David instead of Saul's son, Jonathan.

200 Points. He won both a victory and the people's support with a couple smooth stones.

Correct uestion. Who is King David?

Tidbit. David was the second and greatest king of Israel; his story can be found in First Samuel, chapters 16–31 and Second Samuel. He slew the giant Philistine Goliath with a sling and a rock. He was a great warrior, poet, and musician—credited with writing some of the Psalms.

300 Points. This judge had the most famous haircut in all of the Scriptures, but his strength returned in time to bring down the house.

Correct uestion. Who is Samson?

Tidbit. Samson's story can be found in Judges, chapters 13–16. Samson's strength was ensured as long as his hair remained uncut, but Delilah tricked him and cut his hair, allowing him to be captured by the Philistines. Blinded and forced into slavery, Samson offered a last prayer to God, who gave him the strength to break two supporting pillars, bringing the house down on himself and his enemies.

400 Points. This wise king oversaw the building of the Jerusalem Temple.

Correct uestion. Who is King Solomon?

Tidbit. Solomon was the son of David and Bathsheba, and his story can be found in First Kings, chapters 1–11. He succeeded David to the throne and is credited with many of the sayings in the Book of Proverbs. After his reign ended, the United Kingdom divided into the Northern and Southern Kingdoms.

500 Points. She was the only female judge, who, with another woman, Jael, helped defeat Israel's enemy.

Correct uestion. Who is Deborah?

Tidbit. Deborah's story can be found in Judges, chapters 4–5. The Song of Deborah, in Chapter 5, is regarded as one of the oldest texts in the Bible.

Category: Women to Remember

100 Points. Her yes gave life to the One, who in turn assured life for all.

Correct uestion. Who is Mary, mother of Jesus?

Tidbit. Mary's story is one of trust and faith. She models what God can do for those who are open to God's work in their life.

200 Points. Jacob had to work fourteen years to marry this woman of his dreams, who gave birth to a dreamer in his own right.

Correct uestion. Who is Rachel?

Tidbit. In Genesis, chapters 29–30, Jacob worked seven years to marry Rachel, but was fooled into marrying her sister, Leah, which required him to work seven more years before he could finally marry Rachel. Rachel gave birth to Joseph, whose ability to interpret dreams brought him to the right hand of Pharaoh.

300 Points. Her commitment to her mother-in-law, Naomi, inspired the famous line, "Wherever you go, I will go; wherever you live, I will live." Her book bears her name.

Correct uestion. Who is Ruth?

Tidbit. The Book of Ruth is a great story of faithful love that ends in Ruth's marriage to Boaz. Her great-grandson was King David.

400 Points. She was the first person to see Jesus' empty tomb and was a faithful follower of Jesus.

Correct uestion. Who is Mary Magdalene?

Tidbit. Mary Magdalene was the first to announce that Jesus had been raised from the dead (John 20:1–18), and was likely the leader of a group of women who followed Jesus throughout his ministry and Resurrection.

500 Points. These two women "acted up" in the early church, supporting Paul and teaching about Christianity.

Correct uestion. Who are Lydia and Priscilla?

Tidbit. The inclusion of Lydia and Priscilla in the Acts of the Apostles powerfully demonstrates the important role of women in the early church. They helped Paul in his missionary works, and their stories can be found in Acts of the Apostles 16:14–15 and 18:1–26.

Category: Disciples

100 Points. This disciple "rocked" so much that he was given the keys to the church.

Correct uestion. Who is Peter?

Tidbit. Simon Peter, or Cephas, whose name means "rock," was given that name by Jesus after his declaration of faith in which he proclaimed Jesus as the Son of God, in Matthew 16:13–20. He was also the most well-known and outspoken of the disciples, becoming a strong leader in the early church. He is recognized as the first pope.

200 Points. Without a doubt, this disciple had to see to believe.

Correct uestion. Who is Thomas?

Tidbit. Doubting Thomas is most well-known for doubting the disciples who claimed to have seen the resurrected Jesus (John, chapter 20) and he insisted on touching the nail marks in Jesus' hands and the mark in his side before he would believe. Later in the story, Jesus obliges Thomas, who exclaims, "My Lord and my God!"

300 Points. He was very taxing until Jesus came along and said, "Follow me."

Correct uestion. Who is Matthew?

Tidbit. Matthew's call, found in Matthew 9:9–13, from being a tax collector—a rather despised occupation even then—to being a disciple of Jesus, powerfully shows that Jesus came to save the sinful and befriend the outcast, not to affirm the best and the brightest.

400 Points. For thirty pieces of silver, his good-bye kiss was his last.

Correct uestion. Who is Judas Iscariot?

Tidbit. Judas watched over the money for the disciples. He led the Jewish leaders to Gethsemane after the Last Supper, and betrayed Jesus with a kiss. After Jesus was condemned to die, Judas committed suicide.

500 Points. These sons of thunder were led from their fishing boats to the top of the mountain.

Correct uestion. Who are James and John?

Tidbit. James and John, Zebedee's sons, were nicknamed the Sons of Thunder by Jesus—presumably because of their blustery attitude. They are often mentioned along with Peter as the three disciples most closely connected to Jesus.

Category: Gospel People

100 Points. Being short of stature, he climbed a tree to get a better look and was changed forever by what he saw.

Correct uestion. Who is Zacchaeus?

Tidbit. Zacchaeus was the chief tax collector of Jericho, who climbed a sycamore tree to get a better look at Jesus as he was passing by. Jesus noticed him, called him down, and asked to have dinner with him. Afterward, Zacchaeus offered to give half of all he owned to the poor. His story is found in Luke 19:1–10.

200 Points. Mary and Martha thought he was all wrapped up, until Jesus commanded him to get up.

Correct uestion. Who is Lazarus?

Tidbit. Lazarus was the brother of Martha and Mary, who sent for Jesus to heal Lazarus when he became ill (John 11:1–44). All three were good friends of Jesus. Later, when Jesus heard about Lazarus' death, he wept and then raised Lazarus back to life.

300 Points. Though he was blind as a bat, he could not be kept silent when he heard that the Son of David was nearby.

Correct uestion. Who is Bartimaeus?

Tidbit. Bartimaeus was a blind beggar in Jericho who called out to Jesus to heal him. His story is found in Mark 10:46–52, Matthew 20:29–34, and Luke 18:35–43.

400 Points. She gave birth to a prophet who made a straight path to the Jordan River for Jesus.

Correct uestion. Who is Elizabeth?

Tidbit. Elizabeth was married to Zechariah and was Mary's cousin (Luke 1:39–80). She gave birth to John the Baptist, who baptized Jesus in the Jordan River.

500 Points. Thinking he had done it all, he left saddened that he could not fit his camel through the eye of a needle.

Correct uestion. Who is the rich young man?

Tidbit. The story of the rich young man is found in Matthew 19:16–30, Mark 10:17–31, and Luke 18:18–30. In it, a wealthy young man approaches Jesus with a question about how he can inherit eternal life. Jesus challenges the young man to sell everything and follow him. The man leaves grieving, and Jesus uses the event to talk about the danger of possessions.

Category: Books of the Bible

100 Points. This sequel to Luke tells the story of the early church.

Correct uestion. What is the Acts of the Apostles?

Tidbit. The Acts of the Apostles was written by Luke, who wrote the Gospel of Luke and the Acts of the Apostles as a two-volume set. Acts tells the story of the early church after Jesus' Resurrection. It was written around A.D. 80.

200 Points. This book is the same whether you sing it, say it, or pray it.

Correct uestion. What is the Book of Psalms?

Tidbit. There are 150 Psalms, which are grouped into five categories: hymns of praise, hymns of lament, hymns of wisdom, hymns of worship, and historical psalms. Many were attributed to King David, even though most of them were written after his death.

300 Points. This book leads the reader through burning bushes, plagues, parted waters, dry deserts, and even some stone writing.

Correct uestion. What is the Book of Exodus?

Tidbit. The Book of Exodus tells the story of Israel's liberation from the slavery of Pharaoh to the freedom of a covenant with God. God reveals himself as a burning bush to a prophet named Moses, who eventually leads God's people to freedom.

400 Points. If you want the shortest account of Jesus' life, death, and Resurrection, then read this Gospel.

Correct uestion. What is the Gospel of Mark?

Tidbit. Mark was the first Gospel written, about A.D. 65–70, by a Gentile Christian. The author was trying to tell the story of Jesus to a group of non-Jewish Christians who were experiencing persecution for their belief in Jesus. It is a "short and sweet" Gospel that portrays Jesus as a man of action who calls people into discipleship.

500 Points. What this last book reveals is not the future, but rather the persecution of a young church.

Correct uestion. What is the Book of Revelation?

Tidbit. The Book of Revelation is referred to as apocalyptic literature, that is, literature that uses symbolic, coded language to communicate a message of hope to a persecuted people. The Book of Revelation was written around A.D. 92–96 to Christians who were persecuted by the Roman emperor Domitian. The coded language allowed Christians to understand its message of God's victory over evil (in other words, the Romans).

HOLY WORD SQUARES

Object of the Game

This game show activity is modeled after that perennial favorite *Hollywood S uares*. As in the game ticktacktoe, contestants attempt to be the first player (or team) to get three *X*'s or *O*'s in a row. The three *X*'s or *O*'s can be horizontal, vertical, or diagonal. Players earn the right to get their *X* or *O* on a particular square by accurately deciding whether the guest star in that square has answered a Bible question correctly.

HOW THE GAME IS PLAYED

Players Needed

- ☐ one host (usually the group leader)
- ☐ nine guest stars (see the section entitled "Variations on the Show" if this many guest stars are not available)
- ☐ two contestants

Supplies

- ☐ nine blank name tags made from poster board and safety pins or tape
- ☐ a marker
- ☐ masking tape
- ☐ eleven blank sheets of paper
- ☐ nine copies of "Holy Word Squares—Questions for Guest Stars" (pages 77–79)
- ☐ a coin
- ☐ a Bible for everyone (optional)
- ☐ prizes (optional)

Room Setup

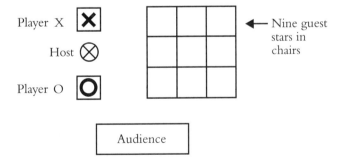

For added effect, invite the first three guest stars to sit on the floor, the next three to sit in chairs behind them, and the last three to stand behind the people in the chairs. This will give the visual effect of a vertical square.

Preparing the Guest Stars

Recruit nine guest stars and give each one a blank name tag and a copy of "Holy Word Squares—Questions for Guest Stars," on pages 77–79. Note that this is a separate handout that doesn't contain the tidbit statements. Meet with the guest stars privately. Have them write their name or the name of a favorite biblical character on the blank name tag. Let them know that every question the host will be asking is printed on the handout you gave them. Each question includes a correct answer and an incorrect answer. They may choose to respond with either one. Encourage them to be humorous with the contestants, even offering an initial response that is not listed on the handout. However, their final response must be one of the two choices on the handout.

Write a large X on nine sheets of paper. Turn the sheets over and write a large O on each one. Give one of these sheets to each guest star. Make two more signs, one marked with a large X and one marked with a large O. Tape these to the floor to mark where you want the contestants to stand.

Game Directions

1. Invite the contestants and the guest stars to stand in their designated spots and introduce the guest stars.

2. Flip a coin to determine which contestant goes first. Be sure it is clear which contestant controls the X's and which contestant controls the O's.

3. Let the first contestant select a guest star. Read aloud for that star one of the questions from the "Holy Word Squares—Questions," on pages 71–76.

4. After the chosen guest star offers a final answer, direct the contestant to state whether the answer is true or false. Announce whether the contestant is correct.

5. If the contestant is correct, the guest star must hold up the mark the contestant is standing on (either an X or an O) for the remainder of the game. If the contestant answers *incorrectly,* the guest star holds up

the opposing player's mark unless the mark would result in a win. Note: A player cannot win the game because of an opposing player's wrong answer.

6. After revealing the correct answer, take a moment to add the corresponding tidbit for the question. If your situation allows it, you may wish to pause and have the contestants and audience members look up the answer in the Bible. Keep in mind that the point of the game is for the young people to learn more about the Scriptures and not just to win.

7. After all the squares have been played, if neither player has three in a row, the winner is the player with the most marks on the board.

8. Give a prize to the winning player if you choose to use prizes.

Variations on the Show

Team play. After designating your guest stars, divide the remaining group into two teams to act as the two contestants. Select a captain for each team. The captain's job is to be the official spokesperson for his or her team.

Guest stars. Recruit highly visible leaders in the parish or school —principals, pastors, parish council presidents, staff members, or other local personalities—to be the guest stars. Reserve the center square for the best known of the personalities who are recruited.

Free-for-all. If you do not have enough people to serve as guest stars, divide the group into two teams, give each team a Bible, and direct the teams to be seated. Mark a ticktacktoe model on the floor or board, and number the squares 1 through 9. Read a question aloud, and let the teams use a Bible to find the answer. When someone thinks that they have the correct answer, they are to stand up and provide an answer immediately. If it is correct, they get to place their mark on any square they wish by calling out the number of the square they want their mark placed on. If their answer is incorrect, the opposing team gets to continue looking for the correct answer. If that team finds the correct answer, they get a mark in the square. If they answer incorrectly, the square remains unmarked and another question is asked.

Numbered squares. If you do not have enough people to serve as guest stars, mark a ticktacktoe model on the floor or on a board, and number the squares 1 through 9. Invite two contestants forward to play. Let the first contestant select a square, and then read aloud the question from "Holy Word Squares—Questions" (pages 71–76) that corresponds to that square's number. Also read aloud one of the two responses. Instruct the contestant to answer true or false. If he or she is correct, award the square.

Invite the next contestant to select a new square from the remaining squares. Read aloud the corresponding question, and so on, until someone wins the game.

HOLY WORD SQUARES—QUESTIONS

1. The first five books of the Bible are also known as what?

Correct answer. the Pentateuch

Incorrect answer. the historical books

Tidbit. *Pentateuch* means "five-part writing." The Jewish faith also refers to these books as the *Torah*, which means "teaching" or "instruction."

2. The story of Moses is found in which book of the Bible?

Correct answer. Exodus

Incorrect answer. Genesis

Tidbit. Moses was the Hebrew who led God's people away from the slavery of Pharaoh and Egypt and to the Promised Land, Canaan.

3. "Blessed are the poor in spirit, for theirs is the kingdom of heaven" is the first verse of which famous saying?

Correct answer. the Beatitudes

Incorrect answer. the Great Commission

Tidbit. The Beatitudes (Matthew 5:1–12, Luke 6:20–26) are teachings that offer ways of thinking and behaving in the world. They introduced what is called the Sermon on the Mount, and Jesus used them to help teach the people what the Reign of God is about.

4. Which of the following books of the Bible is an epistle: Revelation, Tobit, Acts of the Apostles, or Romans?

Correct answer. Romans

Incorrect answer. Revelation

Tidbit. The epistles are letters that were written to the early church after Jesus' Resurrection. Many of the epistles were written by Saint Paul or his followers.

5. Which was the first Gospel written?

Correct answer. Mark

Incorrect answer. Matthew

Tidbit. Matthew is the first Gospel listed in the Bible (written around A.D. 85), but Mark was actually the first, and shortest, to be written (around A.D. 65–70).

6. Of the following four books, which one is not part of the wisdom and poetry books of the Old Testament: Psalms, Esther, Job, or Proverbs?

Correct answer. Esther

Incorrect answer. Job

Tidbit. Esther is one of the historical books.

7. Who did Jesus take with him to the mountain to witness the Transfiguration?

Correct answer. Peter, James, and John

Incorrect answer. Matthew, Mark, and Luke

Tidbit. Peter, James, and John witnessed Jesus' face shining like the sun and the appearance of Moses and Elijah. Moses' presence affirmed Jesus as the fulfillment of the Law. Elijah's presence affirmed Jesus as the fulfillment of the prophets (Matthew 17:1–13).

8. Who were the three major prophets?

Correct answer. Isaiah, Jeremiah, and Ezekiel

Incorrect answer. Micah, Amos, and Hosea

Tidbit. Isaiah, Jeremiah, and Ezekiel are considered the major prophets because their books are long.

9. "A soft answer turns away wrath, but a harsh word stirs up anger" is from which book of the Bible?

Correct answer. Proverbs

Incorrect answer. Judges

Tidbit. The Book of Proverbs is often attributed to Solomon because of his legendary wisdom, but the actual author is unknown. The Book of Proverbs was written from 970–538 B.C.

10. In John's Gospel, what does Jesus do at the Last Supper that does not appear in the other Gospels?

Correct answer. He washes the feet of the disciples.

Incorrect answer. He asks John to watch over his mother, Mary.

Tidbit. The washing of the disciples' feet is the action we remember and celebrate on Holy Thursday each year, as a sign of the type of discipleship Jesus invites all Christians to.

11. The word *gospel* means what?

Correct answer. "good news"

Incorrect answer. "follower of Christ"

Tidbit. The authors of the Gospels wanted to share the big and important news of Jesus Christ with the world.

12. Of the following four people, who was not a prophet: Obadiah, Haggai, Sirach, or Jonah?

Correct answer. Sirach

Incorrect answer. Jonah

Tidbit. The Book of Sirach was written by a wise man named Jesus Ben Sira around 180 B.C. It outlines the superiority of Jewish wisdom over Greek wisdom and is therefore one of the wisdom books.

13. What is the longest book in the Bible?

Correct answer. Psalms

Incorrect answer. Genesis

Tidbit. The Book of Psalms contains 150 psalms divided into five categories: hymns of praise and thanksgiving, hymns of lament or petition, hymns of wisdom, hymns of worship, and historical psalms.

14. The literary form that uses a short story, often with an unusual or shocking ending, to make a spiritual point is called what?

Correct answer. a parable

Incorrect answer. a hyperbole

Tidbit. Jesus often used parables, such as the parable of the prodigal son and the parable of the lost sheep, to teach about God's Reign.

15. What was Paul's name before he encountered the vision of Jesus on the road to Damascus?

Correct answer. Saul of Tarsus

Incorrect answer. Cephas

Tidbit. Paul had a profound moment of conversion as he traveled to Damascus. As a result of his experience, he switched from despising Christians to being one of their greatest leaders and evangelizers.

16. Who is considered to be Israel's greatest king?

Correct answer. David

Incorrect answer. Saul

Tidbit. David was the successor to Saul, and he established Jerusalem as the religious center of Israel, moving the ark of the Covenant there and bringing Israel to its zenith as a nation.

17. Who replaced Judas as the twelfth disciple after Judas hung himself?

Correct answer. Matthias

Incorrect answer. Barnabas

Tidbit. In Acts of the Apostles 1:12–26, Peter leads the disciples in prayer. Then lots are cast to determine which of two people, Joseph or Matthias, will take Judas's place. The lot falls on Matthias.

18. Which Gospel tells the most stories from the time before Jesus' birth?

Correct answer. Luke

Incorrect answer. Matthew

Tidbit. Luke's Gospel, written about A.D. 80, was directed toward Gentile (non-Jewish) Christians and included many stories affirming the dignity of marginalized people such as women, Samaritans, and poor people. Luke's Gospel includes Mary's visitation by the angel Gabriel and her visit with her cousin Elizabeth.

19. The Jordan River connects which two bodies of water?

Correct answer. the Sea of Galilee and the Dead Sea

Incorrect answer. the Mediterranean Sea and the Red Sea

Tidbit. The Jordan River, where John baptized Jesus, was an important source of water and livelihood for many people in the Holy Land.

20. Moses first encountered God where?

Correct answer. in a burning bush

Incorrect answer. at the Red Sea

Tidbit. In Exodus 3:1–12, Moses is instructed by God's voice coming from a burning bush to take off his sandals because he is standing on holy ground (in the presence of God).

21. Who are considered the father and mother in faith of three major world religions: Judaism, Christianity, and Islam?

Correct answer. Abraham and Sarah

Incorrect answer. Moses and Miriam

Tidbit. Abraham and Sarah are considered the founders of what later became the people of Israel. Because Jesus was a Jew, Christians also consider Abraham and Sarah to be their religious ancestors. And Muslims consider themselves to be children of Ishmael who was the son of Abraham and Hagar, a slave of Sarah's.

22. Where was Jesus crucified?

Correct answer. Golgotha

Incorrect answer. Midian

Tidbit. *Golgotha* means "place of the skull." Located just outside Jerusalem, Golgotha was the common site for crucifixions. The Romans wanted everyone to see what happened to those who went against Rome's authority.

23. Which Gospel was written last?

Correct answer. John

Incorrect answer. Luke

Tidbit. The Gospel of John was written from A.D. 90–100. It was addressed to Christians throughout the world, many of whom were being persecuted for their belief in Jesus.

24. The Book of Revelation is what type of writing?

Correct answer. apocalyptic

Incorrect answer. an epistle

Tidbit. The Book of Revelation was written by a Jewish-Christian prophet named John around A.D. 92–96 and was addressed to Christian churches undergoing persecution by Rome. John's writings criticized Roman leadership, so he used a coded language to avoid being arrested. The Book of Revelation was not written to foretell the future, as some have claimed.

25. In the story of Adam and Eve, how is Eve formed?

Correct answer. from the rib of Adam

Incorrect answer. from mud and water

Tidbit. Genesis 2:21–23 says that God put man into a deep sleep and formed woman from one of his ribs. Man later remarked, "This at last is bone of my bones/and flesh of my flesh."

HOLY WORD SQUARES—QUESTIONS FOR GUEST STARS

1. The first five books of the Bible are also known as what?
Correct answer. the Pentateuch
Incorrect answer. the historical books

2. The story of Moses is found in which book of the Bible?
Correct answer. Exodus
Incorrect answer. Genesis

3. "Blessed are the poor in spirit, for theirs is the kingdom of heaven" is the first verse of which famous saying?
Correct answer. the Beatitudes
Incorrect answer. the Great Commission

4. Which of the following books of the Bible is an epistle: Revelation, Tobit, Acts of the Apostles, or Romans?
Correct answer. Romans
Incorrect answer. Revelation

5. Which was the first Gospel written?
Correct answer. Mark
Incorrect answer. Matthew

6. Of the following four books, which one is not part of the wisdom and poetry books of the Old Testament: Psalms, Esther, Job, or Proverbs?
Correct answer. Esther
Incorrect answer. Job

7. Who did Jesus take with him to the mountain to witness the Transfiguration?
Correct answer. Peter, James, and John
Incorrect answer. Matthew, Mark, and Luke

8. Who were the three major prophets?
Correct answer. Isaiah, Jeremiah, and Ezekiel
Incorrect answer. Micah, Amos, and Hosea

9. "A soft answer turns away wrath, but a harsh word stirs up anger" is from which book of the Bible?

Correct answer. Proverbs

Incorrect answer. Judges

10. In John's Gospel, what does Jesus do at the Last Supper that does not appear in the other Gospels?

Correct answer. He washes the feet of the disciples.

Incorrect answer. He asks John to watch over his mother, Mary.

11. The word *gospel* means what?

Correct answer. "good news"

Incorrect answer. "follower of Christ"

12. Of the following four people, who was not a prophet: Obadiah, Haggai, Sirach, or Jonah?

Correct answer. Sirach

Incorrect answer. Jonah

13. What is the longest book in the Bible?

Correct answer. Psalms

Incorrect answer. Genesis

14. The literary form that uses a short story, often with an unusual or shocking ending, to make a spiritual point is called what?

Correct answer. a parable

Incorrect answer. a hyperbole

15. What was Paul's name before he encountered the vision of Jesus on the road to Damascus?

Correct answer. Saul of Tarsus

Incorrect answer. Cephas

16. Who is considered to be Israel's greatest king?

Correct answer. David

Incorrect answer. Saul

17. Who replaced Judas as the twelfth disciple after Judas hung himself?

Correct answer. Matthias

Incorrect answer. Barnabas

18. Which Gospel tells the most stories from the time before Jesus' birth?

Correct answer. Luke

Incorrect answer. Matthew

19. The Jordan River connects which two bodies of water?

Correct answer. the Sea of Galilee and the Dead Sea

Incorrect answer. the Mediterranean Sea and the Red Sea

20. Moses first encountered God where?

Correct answer. in a burning bush

Incorrect answer. at the Red Sea

21. Who are considered the father and mother in faith of three major world religions: Judaism, Christianity, and Islam?

Correct answer. Abraham and Sarah

Incorrect answer. Moses and Miriam

22. Where was Jesus crucified?

Correct answer. Golgotha

Incorrect answer. Midian

23. Which Gospel was written last?

Correct answer. John

Incorrect answer. Luke

24. The Book of Revelation is what type of writing?

Correct answer. apocalyptic

Incorrect answer. an epistle

25. In the story of Adam and Eve, how is Eve formed?

Correct answer. from the rib of Adam

Incorrect answer. from mud and water

THE BIBLE IS RIGHT

C'MON DOWN!

Object of the Game

Modeled after the game show *The Price is Right*, this game begins with four audience members being invited to "come on down" and be contestants. The contestants are asked to answer a numerical question about the Bible. The contestant whose response is closest to the actual answer without going over it, is invited to compete individually in a second round, which tests his or her Bible knowledge. Two rounds of ten questions and answers are provided.

HOW THE GAME IS PLAYED

Players Needed

- ☐ one host
- ☐ four contestants for each set of questions
- ☐ one scribe

Supplies

- ☐ newsprint and markers
- ☐ pencils and slips of paper
- ☐ a basket
- ☐ a clock or watch that counts seconds
- ☐ prizes for winners (optional)
- ☐ a Bible for everyone (optional)

Room Setup

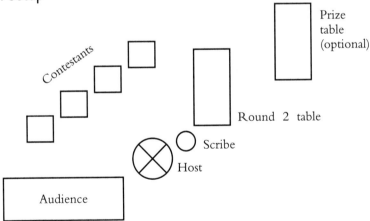

Round Two Setup

Copy the list for each of the round two questions, on pages 88–92, onto a separate sheet of newsprint. Be sure that you do not copy the answers. Keep the lists out of sight near the round two table until the questions are asked. When it is time for each question, post the corresponding list so that all can see, and provide a marker if the question calls for a written response.

Post another sheet of newsprint near the round two table, and provide a marker for recording the round two contestants' names and point totals.

Game Directions

Round One

1. Invite the participants to write their names on a slip of paper and place them in the basket. Read the introductory script from page 84 or use your own words to introduce the game. Then pick the names of four people from the basket and invite those people to "come on down."

2. After the contestants introduce themselves, ask a round one question from pages 85–87. Invite the players to give their answer to the question, beginning with the *last* player called from the audience. Proceed in order to the first person called. Explain that no two contestants may offer the same answer.

3. The player whose response is closest without going over the correct number moves on to round two. If all guesses are higher than the correct answer, the contestants try again until someone comes closest to the correct number without going over.

4. You might want to provide the winner of round one with a small prize such as a bite-size candy bar or a bookmark.

Round Two

1. Invite the winner of round one "onstage" (to the round two table) and give him or her a round two question from pages 88–92 to solve. Round two questions are all timed, so be sure to have the scribe keep track of the elapsed time. Each correct answer is worth 5 or 10 points, as indicated. The contestant's points are totaled and written by the scribe next to his or her name on a posted sheet of newsprint.

2. After the contestant has completed round two, direct her or him to rejoin the audience.

3. Pick another name out of the basket and invite that person to "come on down" to join the other three contestants waiting to win a

chance to go to round two. This person will be the first to respond to the next round one question. Once again, invite the contestant whose answer is closest to the correct answer without going over it to play round two.

4. Continue this cycle until you run out of time. The grand-prize winner is the contestant who gets the most points during his or her turn at round two. Give that person a "grand prize" if you are using prizes. In case of a tie, the grand prize can be shared.

Prizes

If you decide to use prizes, try to secure donations of various prizes from area businesses that are frequented by young people (fast-food restaurants, record stores, amusements parks, bowling alleys, dollar stores, and so on). Also consider offering prizes that the young people can use in their classroom or school (no-homework passes, free-lunch passes, and so on). Separate the donations into grand prizes, round two prizes, and round one prizes. Display them so that all the contestants know the prizes they are competing for.

Variations on the Show

Assistants. Recruit two assistants to bring out the round two questions, deliver prizes, and call out the name of the next contestant to "come on down." Give them biblical names such as Abraham and Sarah, Moses and Elijah, or Mary and Rebecca. Perhaps even ask the assistants to dress as their character.

Group play. To involve the entire group, divide everyone into four or more teams. Label every team with a letter (team A, team B, and so on), and ask each team to select a spokesperson after the team members have discussed the question. Conduct rounds one and two as described in the game directions, treating each team as a single contestant.

INTRODUCTORY SCRIPT

To add some humor and lightheartedness to the game, consider using or adapting the following script to begin:

Good afternoon, and welcome to another edition of "The Bible Is Right!" I'm the star and host of the show, Bob Talker. As you know, this is the show that invites four lucky people from our studio audience (that's you) to "come on down" and try your luck at Bible knowledge and trivia.

There are two rounds to each part of the game. The first round is based on numbers associated with the Bible and will determine the lucky contestant who will be able to stand next to me, your host and star, Bob Talker! Not only that, but that special someone will also get the opportunity to play round two and answer a question with multiple answers based on the Bible. Each round two contestant can score up to 60 points. The round two contestant with the highest score by the end of the show will be declared our grand-prize winner, which means that he or she will get a second chance to stand here next to me, your star and host, Bob Talker! The grand-prize winner will earn a huge round of applause and also take home the grand prize. And now, to begin our show, let's see who our first four contestants will be.

[Pull four names out of the basket, one at a time, announcing each name followed by the words, Come on down; you're the next contestant on "The Bible is Right!"]

THE BIBLE IS RIGHT—QUESTIONS AND ANSWERS

Round One Questions

I. How many books are in a Catholic Bible?

Answer. 73

Tidbit. Catholic Bibles have seven more books than most Protestant Bibles. These books are often referred to as the Apocrypha or Deuterocanonical Books.

2. What year (B.C.) did the Babylonians overtake the Israelites, destroy the Jerusalem Temple, and send the residents into exile?

Answer. 587 B.C.

Tidbit. This was a key event in Old Testament history and many of the prophetic writings refer to it. In fact, many of the later writings found in the Old Testament can be understood only in light of the Babylonian Exile.

3. What year (A.D.) was the Acts of the Apostles written?

Answer. A.D. 80

Tidbit. The author of the Gospel of Luke also wrote the Acts of the Apostles. In fact, the Gospel of Luke and the Acts of the Apostles were originally one book, with the first half highlighting the life of Jesus and the second half highlighting the life of the early church after Jesus' Resurrection.

4. How many chapters are in the Book of Exodus?

Answer. 40

Tidbit. Exodus is the second book of the Bible, and it is the story of Israel's liberation from the slavery and bondage of Egypt and Pharaoh. The Exodus is a central event in Old Testament history, and the central character leading the Hebrew people through it all is Moses.

5. What year (A.D.) was the Second Letter of Peter written?

Answer. A.D. 130

Tidbit. Many scholars think the Second Letter of Peter was the last book written in the New Testament. The author appealed to the authority of the dead Apostle Peter to warn the early Christians about some false teachings that were being spread at that time.

6. What year (B.C.) did King Solomon complete the Temple in Jerusalem?

Answer. 961 B.C. (give or take a few years)

Tidbit. The Jerusalem Temple was the center of worship for the Israelites from 961 B.C. until its destruction in 587 B.C. by the Babylonians. The Temple was later rebuilt but was destroyed again around A.D. 70 by the Romans.

7. How many prophetic books are there in the Old Testament?

Answer. 18

Tidbit. Prophets spoke for God, usually in times of crisis, to offer God's people challenge or comfort, depending on the situation.

8. What year (B.C.) did the Romans conquer the Holy Land?

Answer. 63 B.C.

Tidbit. The Roman occupation was why many Jews were hoping that a messiah would free them from Roman rule and return them to a free and sovereign nation, as in the time of King David.

9. In the Book of Revelation, how many people from the tribes of Israel were sealed on the forehead as servants of God?

Answer. 144,000

Tidbit. The Book of Revelation uses many symbolic numbers. In this case, it probably refers to a chosen multitude too great to count because 144,000 equals 12 (the number of the tribes of Israel) times 12 (the number of apostles) times 1,000. Scholars have different theories about who the 144,000 represents.

10. How many Jewish kings ruled Israel and Judah during Old Testament times?

Answer. 46

Tidbit. Saul, David, and Solomon ruled the United Kingdom. After Solomon's death the kingdom split into Israel in the north and Judah in the south. Another forty-three kings ruled the divided kingdoms over a period of almost 350 years.

Round Two Questions

I. Number these ten biblical events in the order in which they occurred, with 1 being first and 10 being last. You have 60 seconds beginning now! [Award 5 points for each correct answer.]

List
Jesus raises Lazarus from the dead.
Mary visits Elizabeth.
Noah survives the Flood.
Paul converts to Christianity.
David slays Goliath.
Jesus is baptized in the Jordan River.
Jesus calls the disciples.
Moses leads the Hebrews out of Egypt.
Solomon builds the Temple of Jerusalem.
The Babylonians conquer Israel.

Answers
1. Noah survives the Flood.
2. Moses leads the Hebrews out of Egypt.
3. David slays Goliath.
4. Solomon builds the Temple of Jerusalem.
5. The Babylonians conquer Israel.
6. Mary visits Elizabeth.
7. Jesus is baptized in the Jordan River.
8. Jesus calls the disciples.
9. Jesus raises Lazarus from the dead.
10. Paul converts to Christianity.

2. This is a list of the first two letters in the first name of each of the twelve Apostles. You have 60 seconds to name as many Apostles as you can. [Award 5 points for each correct answer.]

List	Answer
Pe	(Simon) Peter
Ja	James (son of Zebedee)
Jo	John (son of Zebedee)
An	Andrew
Ba	Bartholomew (also called Nathanael)
Ja	James (son of Alphaeus)
Ju	Judas Iscariot
Ma	Matthew (also called Levi)
Ph	Philip
Si	Simon the Zealot
Th	Thaddaeus (also called Judas, son of James)
Th	Thomas

3. Answer true if the following couples were married in the Bible, or false if they were not. You have 60 seconds beginning now. [Award 5 points for each correct answer.]

List	Answer
Adam and Eve	True
Jacob and Leah	True
Moses and Miriam	False (Moses and Zipporah)
Abraham and Rebekah	False (Abraham and Sarah)
Jacob and Rachel	True
Judith and Joshua	False (Judith and Manasseh)
Hannah and Eli	False (Hannah and Elkannah)
David and Bathsheba	True
Mary and John	False (Mary and Joseph)
Elizabeth and Zechariah	True

4. Give a word used today for each of the biblical words on this list. You have 60 seconds beginning now. [Award 5 points for each correct answer.]

List	Answer
patriarch	father
looking glass	mirror
swine	pigs
espoused	engaged
shekels and mites	coins or money (such as dimes and quarters)
money changers	bankers
chaff	straw
epistle	letter
sowing	planting
scribe	secretary or librarian

5. Name the New Testament stories that these liturgical feasts and holy days commemorate. You have 60 seconds beginning now. [Award 10 points for each correct answer.]

List	Answer
Epiphany	the coming of the three Magi, or Wise Men, to see the baby Jesus
Palm Sunday	Jesus' triumphant arrival in Jerusalem
Holy Thursday	the Last Supper and the washing of the disciples' feet
Good Friday	the Crucifixion and death of Jesus
Pentecost	the Holy Spirit descending on the disciples as tongues of fire

6. Name each place that is described. You have 60 seconds beginning now. [Award 10 points for each correct answer.]

List	Answer
the city where Solomon built the Temple	Jerusalem
the sea that Moses led the Israelites through	Red Sea
the city where Jesus was born	Bethlehem

the city where Jesus was raised	Nazareth
the mountain where Moses received the 10 Commandments	Mount Sinai

7. You have 60 seconds to write the full names of the books of the Bible represented by the abbreviations in this list. [Award 5 points for each correct answer.]

List	Answer
Gen	Genesis
Mt	Matthew
Eph	Ephesians
Tob	Tobit
Lev	Leviticus
1 Kgs	First Kings
Jn	John
Rev	Revelation
Ezek	Ezekiel
Isa	Isaiah

8. For each book listed, tell whether it is one of the prophetic books in the Old Testament. You have 60 seconds beginning now. [Award 5 points for each correct answer.]

List	Answer
Tobit	No
Hosea	Yes
Isaiah	Yes
Ruth	No
Philemon	No
Ezra	No
Obadiah	Yes
Malachi	Yes
Joshua	No
Baruch	Yes

9. Tell whether each person listed appears in the Old or New Testament. You have 60 seconds beginning now. [Award 5 points for each correct answer.]

List	Answer
Zacchaeus	New
Daniel	Old
Jeremiah	Old
Junia	New
Phoebe	New
Sarah	Old
Barnabas	New
Zechariah	New
Ezekiel	Old
Hannah	Old

10. Number these New Testament stories about Jesus in the order they occurred in Jesus' life. You have 60 seconds beginning now. [Award 10 points for each correct answer.]

List
Jesus prays in the garden of Gethsemane.
Jesus is tempted in the desert.
Peter denies Jesus.
Jesus is transfigured.
Jesus calls his disciples.

Answers
1. Jesus is tempted in the desert.
2. Jesus calls his disciples.
3. Jesus is transfigured.
4. Jesus prays in the garden of Gethsemane.
5. Peter denies Jesus.

THE REAL FORTUNE

Object of the Game

Like in the popular game show *Wheel of Fortune*, contestants attempt to guess the name of a Bible story, a parable, or a phrase from the Scriptures by guessing or purchasing letters in the phrase after they spin a wheel (or roll a die) to see how many points each letter they guess correctly will be worth.

HOW THE GAME IS PLAYED

Players Needed

- ☐ one host
- ☐ three contestants
- ☐ one scribe (scorekeeper)

Supplies

- ☐ a spinner created from page 96 (or a die)
- ☐ a copy of "The Real Fortune—Phrases" pages (100–106) for the scribe
- ☐ prizes for participants (optional)
- ☐ a score sheet for each phrase, created from page 95
- ☐ a Bible for everyone (optional)

Room Setup

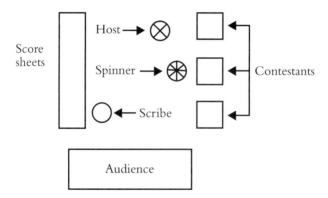

Score Sheet Setup

This game uses puzzles from the section "The Real Fortune—Phrases," on pages 100–106. The phrases are divided into three categories— "Amazing Stories," "Verses to Remember," and "Parables of Jesus."

Category: _____

Score: Incorrect
                                                letters guessed:
Player 1: _____
Player 2: _____
Player 3: _____

Phrase to be solved
(example below)

— — — —   — — —   — — —   — — —
1 2 3 4   5 6 7   8 9 10   11 12 13

Before the game, decide which phrases you will use, and plan to
alternate categories throughout the game.

Use the above model to create a score sheet for each phrase that
you select. Be sure to leave spaces between the words and fill in any
punctuation. The score sheets can be created on newsprint, poster
board, overhead transparencies, a chalkboard, PowerPoint displays, or
whatever works best for you.

Spinner Setup

Copy the wheel from the spinner diagram on page 96 onto heavy
paper and cut it out. Cut a pointer from the same paper. Cut or punch
a ⅛-inch hole in the bottom of the pointer and in the center of the
wheel. Push a round paper fastener through the hole in the pointer and
then through the center of the wheel, and open the fastener so that it
is secure but allows the pointer to spin freely.

If you prefer, omit the spinner and instead provide a die to be
rolled, with the number of dots on the sides of the die corresponding
to the numbered wedges on the wheel. You may want to post a copy of
the spinner for reference.

Game Directions

1. The host selects three contestants and introduces them and the scribe to the audience. The host explains the rules of the game and how the score will be kept.

2. Each contestant spins the spinner (or rolls the die). The contestant with the highest number goes first. The host introduces the phrase

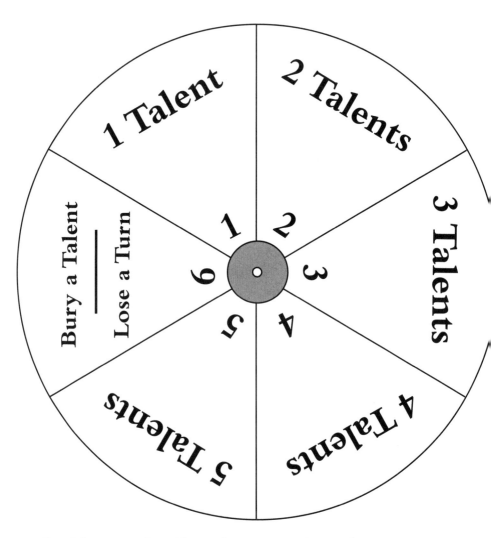

Permission to reproduce this page for program use is granted

to be guessed by calling out its category ("Amazing Stories," "Verses to Remember," or "Parables of Jesus").

3. The first contestant spins the spinner. The contestant then guesses a consonant he or she thinks is in the phrase. If the letter is in the phrase, the scribe writes it in each underlined blank that it appears. The contestant is then awarded a score for that turn, equal to the amount on the spinner multiplied by the number of times the letter is in the phrase. Say the contestant's spin lands on "3 Talents" and the contestant then guesses the letter N. If N appears two times in the phrase, the contestant gets six talents added to his or her score.

4. If a contestant correctly guesses a letter that appears in the phrase, she or he gets to spin and guess again. If she or he guesses a letter that is not in the phrase, the contestant's turn ends and the next contestant gets a turn.

5. If a contestant's spin lands on "Lose a Turn," the contestant loses his or her turn and it becomes the next contestant's turn.

6. A contestant wins by naming the phrase exactly. A contestant may try to guess the phrase at any point during his or her turn. The contestant must first say, "I'd like to solve the phrase," and then state his or her guess. The host announces whether the guess is correct. If it is correct, then the contestant is declared the winner. If it is incorrect, the contestant must sit out until the puzzle is solved correctly by another contestant.

7. Vowels (A, E, I, O and U) cannot be guessed; they must be purchased for three talents each. A contestant may buy a vowel only during his or her turn—either before or after a spin. The contestant says, "I'd like to buy a vowel," and names the vowel. If the vowel is in the phrase, the scribe writes all of its occurrences in the correct blanks. Three talents are subtracted from the contestant's score, no matter how many times the vowel appears. The contestant then may attempt to guess the phrase or spin the spinner.

8. If all the consonants in the phrase have been guessed and only vowels remain, the host indicates that and gives the contestant at the spinner an opportunity to buy a vowel or solve the puzzle. If the contestant is incorrect, it becomes the next contestant's turn.

9. Once a phrase is solved, the winner is joined by two new contestants for a new game with another phrase.

Host Instructions

The host is responsible for beginning the game, introducing the contestants, controlling the flow of the game, declaring a winner, and awarding prizes.

After a puzzle is solved, the host invites everyone to look up the story or phrase in the Bible and asks the winner to read it out loud. The host offers the tidbit information provided with the phrase and any other insights he or she has about the reading.

Scribe Instructions

The scribe writes the correct letters in the appropriate spots and keeps a running score for the contestants on the score sheet. Referring to a copy of "The Real Fortune—Phrases" (pages 100–106), if a contestant guesses a correct letter, the scribe writes it in the appropriate underlined blank or blanks, and then adds the talents earned to the contestant's score on the score sheet. If a contestant guesses an incorrect letter, the scribe writes it on the right-hand side of the score sheet. When a puzzle is solved, the scribe writes in the full answer on the score sheet.

Prizes

If you choose to use prizes, award the winner of each puzzle a medium or large prize and the other two contestants a small prize. Or invite the winner to purchase a prize based on the amount of talents the winner has collected. For example, small prizes might cost between 1 and 10 talents, medium prizes between 11 and 20 talents, and large prizes over 20 talents. Winners could choose to save their talents to add to what they might win in the future in order to purchase a larger prize.

Variations on the Show

Team or family play. Divide the group into three teams of two or three people, or have three families (or parent-child teams) play. Select a captain for each team, who will be the official spokesperson for the team.

Group play. Give everyone in the group a turn spinning the spinner (or rolling the die) and choosing a letter, one person at a time. After a phrase is correctly solved, continue with a new phrase.

The Real Fortune—Phrases

Phrases are divided up into three categories and should be alternated in their use:

- Amazing Stories
- Verses to Remember
- Parables of Jesus

After each answer, the letters used in the phrase are listed. If a letter is used more than once, the number of times it is used is included in parentheses next to the letter.

Category: Amazing Stories

1. *Answer.* N O A H   A N D   T H E   A R K
Letters used. A (3), D, E, H (2), K, N (2), O, R, T
Tidbit. The story of Noah and the ark is found in Genesis, chapters 6–10. It tells how sin corrupted the entire world and how God was forced to cleanse the world from sinful humanity through a huge flood. In the story, God saves the only people who are faithful to him, Noah and his family, by commanding them to build an ark. The Great Flood wipes out all sin so that humanity has another chance to start anew.

2. *Answer.* D A V I D   S L A Y S   G O L I A T H
Letters used. A (3), D (2), G, H, I (2), L (2), O, S (2), T, V, Y
Tidbit. The story of David and Goliath is found in First Samuel, chapter 17, and tells the popular story of the "shot heard round the world" (slingshot, that is). Saul and the Israelite army are in battle against the powerful Philistines. Goliath offers the Israelites a challenge: send their best man out to fight him, and the loser's army will become the servants of the winner's army. David takes up the challenge, but being too small for soldier's armor, he brings with him only a slingshot and a few stones. His first shot hits Goliath in the forehead and knocks him down. David then slays Goliath with Goliath's own sword causing the Philistine army to flee.

3. *Answer.* T H E   T O W E R   O F   B A B E L
Letters used. A, B (2), E (3), F, H, L, O (2), R, T (2), W
Tidbit. The story of the Tower of Babel appears in Genesis 11:1–9 and explains why people are separated by different languages. In the story, all the people of the earth gather to build a tower that reaches to heaven, a symbol of humanity's pride and arrogance. God confuses their language to prevent the completion of the tower.

4. *Answer.* T H E   C R O S S I N G   O F   T H E   R E D   S E A
Letters used. A, C, D, E (4), F, G, H (2), I, N, O (2), R (2), S (3), T (2)
Tidbit. The event that led to the Israelites' crossing the Red Sea to gain their freedom is known as the Exodus, and it is found in Exodus, chapter 14. By miraculously helping the Israelites cross over from the slavery of Egypt to the freedom of the Promised Land, God showed once and for all that he would walk with the people wherever their journey led them.

5. *Answer.* D A N I E L   I N   T H E   L I O N S'   D E N
Letters used. A, D (2), E (3), H, I (3), L (2), N (4), O, S, T
Tidbit. Daniel, chapter 6, describes how jealous rivals of Daniel tricked King Darius into decreeing that it is unlawful to worship any human or god other than the king. The rivals later find Daniel praying to God and turn him in to the king. Even though Daniel is one of King Darius's favorites, the king is forced to uphold the decree, and he puts Daniel in the lion's den to be killed. When the king looks into the den the next morning, Daniel is miraculously unharmed. The king frees Daniel and throws his accusers into the den in his place, where the lions devoured them.

6. *Answer.* J E S U S   W A L K S   O N   W A T E R
Letters used. A (2), E (2), J, K, L, N, O, R, S (3), T, U, W (2)
Tidbit. The story of Jesus walking on water is found in all the Gospels except Luke. It is used to illustrate Jesus' power over the elements of nature, stating clearly that God is bigger and more powerful than any fear or storm that may arise in our life.

7. *Answer.* J E S U S   F E E D S   F I V E   T H O U S A N D

Letters used. A, D (2), E (4), F (2), H, I, J, N, O, S (4), T, U (2), V

Tidbit. The story of Jesus feeding five thousand appears in all four Gospels, which indicates its importance. The story begins with a hungry crowd (hungry both for Jesus' words and for bread to sustain them), and Jesus asks his disciples to see how much food is available. They return with only five loaves and two fish. Jesus blesses the food and invites his disciples to distribute it to the crowd. All the people are fed, and twelve baskets of leftovers are collected.

8. *Answer.* L A Z A R U S   I S   R A I S E D   F R O M   T H E   D E A D

Letters used. A (4), D (3), E (3), F, H, I (2), L, M, O, R (3), S (3), T, U, Z

Tidbit. The raising of Lazarus from the dead appears in John 11:1–44 and gives us insight into the emotions of Jesus as well as his power over death (a prelude to what will happen shortly in Jesus' own death and Resurrection). Lazarus, the brother of Martha and Mary and a close friend of Jesus', dies. On hearing the news, Jesus sheds tears of grief. Jesus' full power is revealed when he asks that the stone be rolled away from Lazarus's tomb. Jesus commands the dead Lazarus to come out. Lazarus does as commanded, amazing everyone.

9. *Answer.* T H E   E M P T Y   T O M B

Letters used. B, E (2), H, M (2), O, P, T (3), Y

Tidbit. No other story in the Bible rivals the Resurrection of Jesus from the dead. This event serves as the hallmark of Christian faith and hope. Through the Resurrection, life overcame death and our sins were forgiven. Humankind was made right with God, once and for all. It is this glorious event that Catholic Christians remember each Sunday at the Eucharist and that is celebrated on Easter Sunday, the high point of the Catholic church's liturgical year.

10. *Answer.* T U R N I N G   W A T E R   I N T O   W I N E

Letters used. A, E (2), G, I (3), N (4), O, R (2), T (3), U, W (2)

Tidbit. The miracle of water turned into wine, found in John 2:1–11, occurred at a wedding feast at Cana, north of Galilee. It is Jesus' first miracle in John's Gospel. It suggests that Jesus was ushering in the time of promise, or "the messianic age," which is often symbolized in prophetic language by overflowing wine. John used this story to declare to all people that God is present to us in and through Jesus.

Category: Verses to Remember

1. *Answer.* G I V E   U S   T H I S   D A Y   O U R   D A I L Y
B R E A D

Letters used. A (3), B, D (3), E (2), G, H, I (3), L, O, R (2), S (2), T, U (2), V, Y (2)

Tidbit. This familiar line from the Lord's Prayer is found in Matthew 6:11 and challenges each of us to trust in God for the necessities of life. By asking only for daily bread, Jesus also seems to be challenging us to use and consume only what we need to sustain life and to not give in to materialism and overconsumption, which may cause others to have less than they need.

2. *Answer.* MY   G O D ,   MY   G O D ,   W H Y   H A V E
Y O U   F O R S A K E N   M E ?

Letters used. A (2), D (2), E (3), F, G (2), H (2), K, M (3), N, O (4), R, S, U, V, W, Y (4)

Tidbit. This famous line from Mark 15:34 has Jesus quoting Psalm 22 as he is dying on the cross. Abandoned by most of his followers, beaten, mocked, ridiculed, and finally nailed to a cross, Jesus is using his last ounce of life to utter a final prayer to God. Even though his words show Jesus' very human feelings of abandonment, they also show Jesus' ultimate faith in God—because all faithful Jews would know that Psalm 22 is ultimately a prayer of hope in God's deliverance.

3. *Answer.* Y O U S H A L L L O V E Y O U R
N E I G H B O R A S Y O U R S E L F

Letters used. A (2), B, E (3), F, G, H (2), I, L (4), N, O (5), R (3), S (3), U (3),V, Y (3)

Tidbit. In Matthew 22:39, we find the heart of Jesus' message, which, along with the commandment to love God with your whole heart, soul, and mind, sums up the Good News that Jesus came to bring. Many of those hearing Jesus' words no doubt thought his definition of neighbor meant only people belonging to your own family or nation. But in the parable about the good Samaritan, Jesus made it clear that all people are our neighbors, even those we might despise.

4. *Answer.* Y O U A R E T H E L I G H T O F T H E
W O R L D

Letters used. A, D, E (3), F, G, H (3), I, L (2), O (3), R (2),T (3), U, W,Y

Tidbit. This remark made by Jesus during his Sermon on the Mount (Matthew 5:14) lets would-be followers of Jesus know that disciples are responsible for bringing light to the darkness in the world. Jesus expects his disciples to bring God's love to bear on sinful situations.

5. *Answer.* I W I L L P O U R O U T M Y S P I R I T

Letters used. I (4), L (2), M, O (2), P (2), R (2), S,T (2), U (2),W, Y

Tidbit. This verse from Acts of the Apostles 2:17 occurs on Pentecost, the day the fire of the Holy Spirit came upon the disciples, who had been hiding in fear for their lives after Jesus' Crucifixion. Pentecost is also known as the birthday of the church because it marks the day the disciples began to do what Jesus had asked them to do—go out and preach the Good News to the ends of the earth. From that day forward, the disciples formed a community of people who believed in Jesus, the risen Christ.

Category: Parables of Jesus

1. *Answer.* T H E   W E D D I N G   B A N Q U E T
Letters used. A, B, D (2), E (3), G, H, I, N (2), Q, T (2), U, W
Tidbit. The parable of the wedding banquet is found in Matthew 22:1–14 and was used by Jesus to help his listeners imagine what the Reign of God will be like. In the parable, those who were invited first, most likely symbolizing religious leaders, choose not to accept the king's invitation to the wedding banquet. So the king extends the invitation to all, including sinners, prostitutes, tax collectors, and the like. Jesus is opening the doors of the Reign of God to anyone, whatever their station in life, who will respond to God's invitation.

2. *Answer.* T H E   G O O D   S A M A R I T A N
Letters used. A (3), D, E, G, H, I, M, N, O (2), R, S, T (2)
Tidbit. The parable of the good Samaritan (Luke 10:30–37) was told by Jesus to show how far one must go to be a disciple. Jesus chose the hero in the story to be a Samaritan, a member of the cultural group that was despised and ridiculed by the Jews of that time. In this parable, love of neighbor goes well beyond city limits and blood ties, to include all people.

3. *Answer.* T H E   P R O D I G A L   S O N
Letters used. A, D, E, G, H, I, L, N,O (2), P, R, S, T
Tidbit. The prodigal son (Luke 15:11–32) beautifully illustrates the outrageous love God has for us. In the story, the father (who represents God) is completely unconcerned for his own dignity and public image in welcoming back his lost younger son. His older son (who represents most law-abiding, common-sense people) was used by Jesus to explain that God wants to save not only those who remain good and faithful but also those who have lost their way in sin and despair.

4. *Answer.* <u>T H E</u>   <u>R I C H</u>   <u>M A N</u>   <u>A N D</u>   <u>L A Z A R U S</u>
Letters used. A (4), C, D, E, H (2), I, L, M, N (2), R (2), S, T, U, Z

Tidbit. This parable (Luke 16:19–31) was used by Jesus to teach people about the proper use of wealth. A rich man ignores the hungry and poor Lazarus on earth. After they both die, a reversal of fortune lands Lazarus in heaven (in the bosom of Abraham) and the rich man in hell. The rich man, wanting to warn his family of what awaits if they do not change their ways, is reminded that plenty of prophets and teachers already have warned against selfishness and greed. This teaching challenged the view held by many people, that wealth was a sign of God's favor.

5. *Answer.* <u>T H E</u>   <u>S O W E R</u>   <u>A N D</u>   <u>T H E</u>   <u>S E E D</u>
Letters used. A, D (2), E (5), H (2), N, O, R, S (2), T (2), W

Tidbit. The parable of the sower and the seed is found in each of the synoptic gospels (Matthew 13:3–8,18–23; Mark 4:3–9,14–20; Luke 8:5–8,11–15) and is used to introduce the meaning and power of parables. The parable also illustrates the different responses people have to the word of God in their life. Some choose to hear it and ignore it, others try it for a while and give up because it is too difficult, and still others let other voices overpower God's word. Finally it shows that the work of faithful disciples who hear the word and put it into practice each day will be multiplied.

Permission to reproduce this page for program use is granted.

BIBLE BASEBALL

Object of the Game

This game is modeled after the game of baseball. The group or class is divided into two opposing teams and a group leader or teacher acts as the pitcher for both sides. The pitcher "throws" a question at each batter. Each correct answer is treated as a base hit, and each incorrect response is an out. Runs and innings are scored according to the regular rules of baseball, with the pitcher throwing an occasional "home run" to give the team at bat a chance to clear the bases.

HOW THE GAME IS PLAYED

Players Needed

☐ one pitcher (the group leader or teacher)
☐ two teams (each comprising half of the entire group or class)
☐ one scribe (scorekeeper)

Supplies and Setup

☐ a scoreboard (see setup instructions, page 109)
☐ a Bible for everyone (optional)
☐ prizes for the winning team (optional)

Room Setup

Set up the room according to the diagram below, using chairs or corners of the room to designate home plate, first base, and so on.

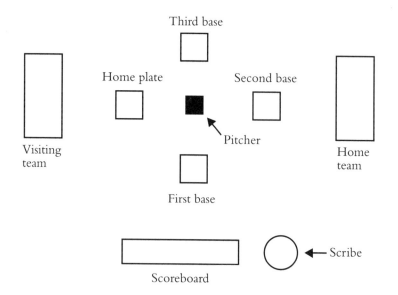

Scoreboard Setup

Provide materials so that the scribe can create the following scoreboard on a chalkboard or an overhead transparency. The markings shown should be permanent, and the outs and runs should be erasable so the scribe can update them as necessary.

		Innings							
Outs		1	2	3	4	5	6	7	
1 2 3	Visiting Team								
1 2 3	Home Team								

Game Directions

1. Select one person to be the scribe (scorekeeper), and ask that person to set up the scoreboard as shown above. Divide the remainder of the group or class into two teams, and assign one person to be the "coach" of each team. Explain that this person is to establish the team's batting order, that is, the order in which the people on the team will go to "bat" by answering a question "thrown" to them by the pitcher (the group leader or teacher). Encourage each team to develop a name rooted in the Scriptures such as the Babylonian Exiles, the Jordan River Rats, or the Ten Plagues.

2. The pitcher flips a coin to see which team bats first. The team winning the toss bats first. The visiting team sits behind home plate, and the home team sits in the "field." The first batter steps up to home plate, and the pitcher asks a question from "Bible Baseball—Questions and Answers," on pages 111–120. Only the batter may answer the question. If the batter gives an incorrect answer or a teammate offers an answer or a hint, the batter is counted out and the next batter is up. If the batter gives the correct answer, it is counted as a hit, and the batter moves to first base and any other players on base move forward one base. Every time a player moves to home plate, the team scores a run. Some of the Bible Baseball questions are marked with an asterisk.

Those are home run questions. If they are answered correctly, the batter and everyone on a base moves to home plate, all scoring runs.

3. After three outs the batting team's half of the inning is over and the teams change sides.

4. The scribe keeps tracks of the outs and total runs for each inning. When time is up or the teams have finished seven innings, the team with the most runs is declared the winner.

Variations on the Game

Team-developed questions. Instead of acting as pitcher and using the questions provided, direct the teams to develop their own questions and answers. Play the game as directed, except invite the members of the nonbatting team to take turns pitching the questions to the batters. This works best if an assigned section of the Bible is used to help narrow the field of questions and keep them applicable to what the young people are learning or reviewing.

Test or review. This game can be adapted for a test or chapter review. If the teacher's manual contains sample test questions, they can easily be used as the questions the pitcher "throws" to the batters.

Tournament. If you have a large group, divide it into four or more teams and sponsor a tournament in which the teams play one another over the course of a few days or several weeks. Offer the team with the best record a group prize or award.

BIBLE BASEBALL—QUESTIONS AND ANSWERS

Old Testament Questions

★ *Indicates a "home run" uestion.*

1. The first five books of the Bible are referred to as what?
Answer. Pentateuch, Torah, or Books of Moses

2. What book of the Bible is a collection of religious songs once attributed solely to David but now attributed to a number of authors?
Answer. Psalms

3. Haggai, Zechariah, Jeremiah, and Joel are what type of books?
Answer. prophetic books

★4. The Decalogue is also known as what?
Answer. the Ten Commandments

5. Founders of the Jewish faith such as Abraham, Isaac, and Jacob are known as what?
Answer. patriarchs

6. The City of David is also named what?
Answer. Jerusalem, also accept Bethlehem

7. Who was the leader of the Exodus?
Answer. Moses

8. Which son did Rebekah favor more, Jacob or Esau?
Answer. Jacob

★9. During what major event in the life of Israel was much of the Old Testament, including Genesis, written and put in final form?
Answer. the Babylonian exile

10. Who was tricked into marrying two sisters, Leah and Rachel?
Answer. Jacob

11. What frightening thing did God ask Abraham to do in order to test his faith?
Answer. sacrifice his only son, Isaac

12. What did Jacob give to his son Joseph?
Answer. a long robe with sleeves (popularly referred to as the coat of many colors)

★13. The twelve sons of Jacob became the founding fathers of what?
Answer. the twelve tribes of Israel

14. What did God do to confuse the people in the story of the Tower of Babel?
Answer. God mixed up their languages so that they could not understand one another.

15. The Jewish day of rest is referred to as what?
Answer. the Sabbath

16. To what land did Moses lead the Israelites after leaving Egypt?
Answer. Canaan

17. What name did God use when speaking with Moses at the burning bush?
Answer. I Am Who I Am

18. Who went with Moses to speak to Pharaoh?
Answer. Aaron, Moses' brother

★19. What prevented the angel of God from striking down the first-born in the Hebrew homes during the tenth plague?
Answer. the blood of a lamb placed over the doorpost

20. During the Exodus, God accompanied the Hebrews throughout the day as a cloud and throughout the night as what?
Answer. a pillar of fire

21. Who raised Moses as an Egyptian prince?
Answer. Pharaoh's daughter

22. What sea did the Israelites cross to escape Pharaoh's army?
Answer. the Red Sea, or Sea of Reeds

23. What happened to the first set of stone tablets containing the Ten Commandments?
Answer. Moses threw them down in anger after Aaron led the people in worshiping a golden calf.

★24. What is the name of the mountain where God gave the Ten Commandments to Moses?
Answer. Mount Sinai

25. A seder is a ritual meal that celebrates what event for the Jews?
Answer. the exodus from slavery to freedom

26. Who led the Israelites into the Promised Land of Canaan?
Answer. Joshua

27. The whole collection of laws from Exodus through Deuteronomy is called what?
Answer. the Mosaic Law or Law of Moses

★28. The Day of Atonement, a holy day for Jews, is also known as what?
Answer. Yom Kippur

29. What is one thing that occurs during a Jubilee year?
Answer. Any one of these: debts are forgiven, land is returned to the original owners, the land is rested and slaves are freed

30. What city in Canaan did Joshua overtake?

Answer. Jericho, which the Israelites circled seven times while blowing rams' horns.

31. Did the period of the Judges occur before or after the time of King David and King Solomon?

Answer. before

32. Who was Hannah's son: Samuel, Isaac, or Solomon?

Answer. Samuel

33. Samson, Gideon, Samuel, and Deborah were all considered what?

Answer. Judges

34. Ruth, a poor Moabite widow, ended up being the great-grandmother of what famous leader?

Answer. King David

35. What army did Samson fight against?

Answer. the Philistines

*★**36.** Who was the first king of Israel?

Answer. Saul

37. What king is responsible for defeating the Philistines and unifying the Israelite tribes into one kingdom?

Answer. King David

38. Which king of Israel was the son of David and Bathsheba?

Answer. Solomon

39. Who was Saul's son and David's best friend?

Answer. Jonathan

40. Who oversaw the building of the Jerusalem Temple?

Answer. King Solomon

★41. In what natural phenomenon did Elijah hear God speaking to him at Horeb?

Answer. a gentle breeze

42. What was unusual about Gomer, the wife of the prophet Homer?

Answer. She was a prostitute.

43. Which of these is not one of the prophetic books: Isaiah, Judith, Micah, or Amos?

Answer. Judith

44. What prophet was thrown into the lion's den?

Answer. Daniel

45. Why did the king order Shadrach, Meshach, and Abednego thrown into a fiery furnace?

Answer. They refused to bow down and worship a false god.

★46. During the Exile, what country were the Israelites forced to stay in?

Answer. Babylonia

47. The Song of Songs is a book of what?

Answer. love poems

48. Which prophet is swallowed by a fish before he does God's work?

Answer. Jonah

49. How many psalms are there in the Book of Psalms?

Answer. 150

★50. What is one type or style of psalm?

Answer. Any one of these: praise or thanksgiving, lament, wisdom, worship (liturgical), historical

New Testament Questions

Indicates a "home run" question.

1. Name the four Gospels in the order in which they appear in the New Testament.

Answer. Matthew, Mark, Luke, and John

2. The Jewish feast of Pentecost, also known as the feast of Weeks, commemorated what Old Testament event?

Answer. God giving the Law to Moses, or God's Covenant with Israel

3. What group during Jesus' time believed that the way to Jewish independence was through a military overthrow of the Romans?

Answer. the Zealots

4. Name the three synoptic Gospels.

Answer. Matthew, Mark, and Luke

5. Which group was more religiously conservative, the Pharisees or the Sadducees?

Answer. the Sadducees

*6. What was the common job title of the despised men also known as publicans?

Answer. tax collectors

7. Which was the first Gospel to be written?

Answer. Mark

8. What was the official governing body of the Jews called?

Answer. the Sanhedrin

9. Which Gospel describes Jesus as the Word made flesh?

Answer. John

10. Who prepared the way for Jesus' ministry by preaching repentance of sins?
Answer. John the Baptist

★11. Who was the mother of John the Baptist?
Answer. Elizabeth

12. Who was the brother of Mary and Martha that Jesus brought back to life?
Answer. Lazarus

13. Which was the last Gospel to be written?
Answer. John

14. Who sentenced Jesus to death?
Answer. Pontius Pilate

★15. Which two Apostles are known as the Sons of Thunder and were Zebedee's sons?
Answer. James and John

16. Who is known as the first martyr for his faith?
Answer. Stephen, who was stoned to death

17. Which Apostle tried to walk on water with Jesus?
Answer. Peter

18. What is the name of the hill Jesus was crucified on?
Answer. Golgotha, or "skull place"

19. What two seas does the Jordan River connect?
Answer. the Sea of Galilee and the Dead Sea

20. What city was Jesus born in?
Answer. Bethlehem

21. Where did Jesus go to pray with his disciples after the Last Supper?
Answer. the garden of Gethsemane

22. What was Jesus' hometown?
Answer. Nazareth

★23. In John's Gospel, what was Jesus' first miracle?
Answer. turning water into wine at a wedding feast in Cana

24. What two people passed by a beaten man in the parable of the Good Samaritan?
Answer. a priest and a Levite

25. What was the name of the tax collector who had to climb a tree to see Jesus?
Answer. Zacchaeus

26. How many years did Jesus' public ministry last?
Answer. three

27. What line from Psalm 22 did Jesus cry out while on the cross?
Answer. "My God, my God, why have you forsaken me?"

28. Who was the first person to discover the empty tomb of Jesus?
Answer. Mary Magdalene

29. Which disciple doubted that Jesus had been raised from the dead?
Answer. Thomas

★30. Which epistle, or letter, is considered Paul's theological or teaching masterpiece?
Answer. the Letter to the Romans

31. Who wrote the Acts of the Apostles?
Answer. Luke

32. What were the first disciples doing when Jesus invited them to follow him?

Answer. fishing

33. Finish this saying: "Blessed are the poor in spirit . . . "

Answer. "for theirs is the kingdom of heaven."

34. What is the Golden Rule?

Answer. Do unto others as you would have them do unto you.

★35. Who was selected to replace Judas as the twelfth Apostle?

Answer. Matthias

36. What is the New Testament book of apocalyptic literature called?

Answer. Revelation

37. What was Paul's name before his conversion?

Answer. Saul (of Tarsus)

38. On what Jewish feast did Jesus celebrate the Last Supper in the Gospel of John?

Answer. Passover

39. How many times did Peter deny Jesus?

Answer. three

40. Who is known as the Beloved Disciple?

Answer. John

41. What happened to Zechariah when he did not believe the angel's news that his wife would bear a son in her old age?

Answer. He was struck mute until his son, John the Baptist, was born.

42. Which Gospel is the shortest?

Answer. Mark

43. What nationality was the woman at the well whom Jesus spoke to in the Gospel of John?

Answer. Samaritan

★44. What was the name of the high priest who wanted Jesus put to death?

Answer. Caiaphas

45. What did Matthew do before he was called to follow Jesus?

Answer. collected taxes

46. What did Jesus tell the rich young man to do in order to gain eternal life?

Answer. sell all he had and give the money to the poor, and then follow Jesus

47. What feast is often called the birthday of the church?

Answer. Pentecost

★48. What happened to Peter when he was first put in prison by King Herod?

Answer. An angel appeared and helped him escape.

49. What did Judas do after betraying Jesus?

Answer. hung himself

50. Which Gospel contains Mary's Magnificat?

Answer. Luke

SCRIPTIONARY

Object of the Game

This game is similar to the board game *Pictionary*. In this version, team members are given a word or phrase that describes a biblical event, story, person, or book. The other members of the team must guess what is being drawn, in the allotted time.

HOW THE GAME IS PLAYED

Players Needed

- ☐ two or more teams of at least two people each
- ☐ one leader, who also is the scorekeeper

Supplies

- ☐ a separate easel and newsprint for each team or a chalkboard big enough so that each team has a section to draw on
- ☐ markers or chalk
- ☐ a watch or clock that displays seconds
- ☐ one die
- ☐ slips of paper, and a pen or pencil
- ☐ prizes for the winning team (optional)
- ☐ a Bible for everyone (optional)

Game Directions

1. The leader divides the group into teams of at least two players each. Up to four teams may play at one time, but more than four is not recommended. Each team must decide the order in which its members will take a turn at drawing. Every member of the team must take a turn at drawing before another member draws again.

2. The leader invites the team with the member who possesses the longest last name to go first. The leader asks someone from the team to roll the die. If an even number comes up, the round is considered an "all-play" round (indicated by an asterisk on pages 125–127), which means that one person from each team draws simultaneously and all the teams try to guess what is being drawn. If the die comes up as an odd number, only the person who rolled the die gets to draw and only that person's team is allowed to call out guesses. Each number on the die corresponds to a particular Scriptionary category, as follows:

If the die reads . . .	The category is . . .
1	Gospel events
★2	miracle stories
3	parables
★4	people's names
5	Pentateuch events
★6	books of the Bible

★ indicates an "all-play" category

3. The leader locates the category in the "Scriptionary—Words and Phrases," on pages 125–127, picks a word or phrase from that category, and writes it on a slip of paper. The leader shows the word or phrase on the slip to the person or persons drawing, and when they are ready, gives the signal to begin.

4. Those who are drawing must remain silent and cannot draw letters or numbers. If a team member guesses a part of a word or phrase that makes up the correct answer, the person or persons drawing may write that part on the newsprint or board and even draw one or more lines before or after it to indicate where it fits in the complete answer. For example, if the phrase being drawn is "walking on water" and someone guesses "water," the person drawing may write on the board, "_____ __ Water"

5. Those who are drawing are given 1 minute to illustrate their event, story, person, or book. The leader must listen very carefully for the first person to correctly guess the answer. If a form of the answer is given, but is not exactly right, the leader should wait until someone says the exact form. At that point, the leader stops the drawing, checks the time, and awards points to the team with the correct answer. If the correct answer is not given within 1 minute, no points are scored. Scoring is as follows:

- Correct answers in an all-play round: 10 points
- Corrrect answers in a single-play round: 5 points
- Incorrect or no answer in any round: 0 points

6. After a word or phrase is guessed correctly, the leader invites the players to share what they know about the event, story, person, or book of the Bible. If a word or phrase is not guessed, the leader offers hints to help the group guess the correct answer. If there is time, the leader invites each team to find a Bible passage that refers to the word or phrase, and asks someone to read it aloud to the group.

7. The opportunity to roll the die and play alone continues in a clockwise fashion through all the teams. This is true even if an even number (an all-play round) is rolled. No matter which team answers the all-play round correctly, the team to the left of the team that rolled the die for that turn goes next.

8. The leader keeps track of each team's score. After the allotted time or number of rounds, the leader declares the team with the highest score the winner and passes out prizes if they are being used.

Variations on the Show

Single player. Instead of playing team against team, invite group members to the board one at a time and show them the word or phrase. Have the person at the board draw the word or phrase until the group guesses. Record times and see who can get the fastest guess.

Reverse Scriptionary. Have one or more people go to the board and while their backs are turned, show the rest of the group the word or phrase. Then have the group direct the people drawing by using shapes and sizes and directions until the people drawing can guess what the word or phrase is. Tell those describing the word that they cannot use the actual phrases or words. For example, if the phrase is "walking on water," group members cannot say, "Draw water" or "Draw Jesus walking." Instead they need to say, "Draw wavy lines across the board," and so on.

SCRIPTIONARY—WORDS AND PHRASES

★Indicates an "all-play" category.

Category 1: Gospel Events

birth of Jesus
calling of the disciples
temptations in the desert
Sermon on the Mount
Crucifixion
cleansing of the Temple
baptism of Jesus
Transfiguration
Resurrection
triumphal entry into Jerusalem

★Category 2: Miracle Stories

healing the blind
parting of the Red Sea
healing the ten lepers
healing of the paralytic
feeding the five thousand
walking on water
huge catch of fish
raising of Lazarus
calming the storm
curing the centurion's servant

Category 3: Parables

good Samaritan
lost sheep
mustard seed
persistent widow
sower and the seed
prodigal son
wedding banquet
sheep and the goats
rich man and Lazarus
Pharisee and the tax collector

★Category 4: People's Names

Joseph
King David
Abraham
Samson
Mary, mother of Jesus
Peter
Moses
Isaac
Mary Magdalene
King Solomon

Category 5: Pentateuch Events

Abraham sacrifices Isaac
ten plagues
burning bush
Ten Commandments
Adam and Eve
fall of Jericho
Exodus
Tower of Babel

Noah and the ark
Creation story

★Category 6: Books of the Bible

Matthew
Revelation
Romans
Isaiah
1 Kings
Genesis
Proverbs
Psalms
Ruth
Acts of the Apostles